CONTENTS

Chapter 1 About Depression

Chapter 2 Depression and Young People

Chapter 3 Diagnosis and Treatment

OTHER TITLES IN THE ISSUES SERIES

For more on these titles, visit: www.independence.co.uk

EXPLORING THE ISSUES

Photocopiable study guides to accompany the above publications. Each four-page A4 guide provides a variety of discussion points and other activities to suit a wide range of ability levels and interests.

A note on critical evaluation

Because the information reprinted here is from a number of different sources, readers should bear in mind the origin of the text and whether the source is likely to have a particular bias when presenting information (just as they would if undertaking their own research). It is hoped that, as you read about the many aspects of the issues explored in this book, you will critically evaluate the information presented. It is important that you decide whether you are being presented with facts or opinions. Does the writer give a biased or an unbiased report? If an opinion is being expressed, do you agree with the writer?

Coping with Depression offers a useful starting point for those who need convenient access to information about the many issues involved. However, it is only a starting point. Following each article is a URL to the relevant organisation's website, which you may wish to visit for further information.

Depression

Everyone experiences variation in mood: sometimes you just feel a bit low, or experience normal grief that accompanies the loss of someone you love. But a long-lasting low mood that interferes with the ability to function, feel pleasure or take an interest in things is not merely a case of the blues – it is an illness known as depression. This article looks at the symptoms, causes and possible treatments for depression.

Key points

⇨ Symptoms of depression include a long-lasting unhappy mood, low self-esteem, and lack of motivation.

⇨ Depression comes in different forms from mild, moderate and severe to psychotic in some rare cases. Part of bipolar disorder may also involve periods of depression.

⇨ Different factors are thought to contribute to depression, such as genetics, brain chemistry, upbringing and lifestyle.

⇨ Depression can be treated with either medication, therapy or both.

If you think you are suffering from depression speak to your GP who can prescribe medication or refer you to a counsellor.

Depression affects a person's physical state, mood and thought processes. People with depression cannot merely 'pull themselves together' and get better. It is not a sign of personal weakness or a condition that can be willed away but an illness that needs treatment to reduce symptoms.

Depression affects anyone of any age, including young children. According to the Mental Health Foundation, one in six people will have depression at some point in their life. It is most common in people aged 25 to 44 years. However, these figures are based on people who actually seek help, and there will be more who remain undiagnosed. People who do not receive support, especially young men, are at particular risk of suicide.[1]

Symptoms of depression

Listed below are a number of symptoms associated with depression. Not everyone who is depressed will experience every symptom. Some people experience a few symptoms, some experience many. Severity of symptoms varies between individuals and also varies over time.

⇨ Feelings of helplessness and hopelessness.

⇨ Feeling useless, inadequate, bad.

⇨ Self-hatred, constant questioning of thoughts and actions, an overwhelming need for reassurance.

⇨ Being vulnerable and 'over-sensitive'.

⇨ Feeling guilty.

⇨ A loss of energy and motivation, that makes even the simplest tasks or decision seem difficult.

RETHINK

⇨ Self-harm.

⇨ Loss or gain in weight.

⇨ Difficulty with getting off to sleep, or (less frequently) an excessive desire to sleep.

⇨ Agitation and restlessness.

⇨ Loss of sex drive.

⇨ Finding it impossible to concentrate for any length of time, forgetfulness and a sense of unreality.

⇨ Physical aches and pains, sometimes with the fear that you are seriously ill.

Severe depression significantly interferes with an individual's ability to cope with their daily life

In more serious cases of depression, these feelings may also include:

⇨ suicidal ideas;

⇨ failure to eat or drink;

⇨ delusions and/or hallucinations.

What are the different types of depression?

Depression can come in different forms and in different degrees. For the purpose of management and treatment, the most common types of depression are often referred to as the following:[2]

Mild: Depression is described as mild when it has a negative but limited effect on your daily life; for example, you may have difficulty concentrating at work or motivating yourself to do the things you normally enjoy.

Moderate: More of the symptoms are present in moderate depression than in mild depression and they are usually more obvious. There may be a clear reduction in functioning at home and in the workplace.

Severe (sometimes known as clinical or major depression): Severe depression significantly interferes with an individual's ability to cope with their daily life – eating, sleeping and many other everyday activities seem impossible tasks which can be life threatening as a person may be unable to look after themselves. There is also a high risk of suicide. Some people may experience only one episode but several episodes in a lifetime is more common. In some circumstances, a person's inability to function can lead to hospitalisation.

Less common types of depression include:

Bipolar Disorder (manic depression): This is also a less common form of depression and characterised by cyclical mood changes of severe highs (mania) and lows (depression).

Psychotic depression: This occurs in rare cases of severe depression when depressive symptoms are accompanied by some form of psychosis such as hallucinations or delusions.

Post-natal depression: This is not 'the baby blues' which occurs two to three days after the birth and goes away. Post-natal depression can occur from about two weeks and up to a year after the birth. Around one in every ten women has post-natal depression after having a baby.[3]

Seasonal affective disorder (SAD): A type of depression linked to exposure to sunlight, which generally coincides with the approach of winter, starting usually from September and lasting until spring brings longer days and more sunshine. Symptoms of this depression are a desire to sleep more and eat carbohydrate foods. Bright light therapy can be helpful.

What causes depression?

There is no single known cause of depression. Current explanations tend to lie in a combination of brain chemistry, genetic and environmental factors.[4]

Biochemical

It is known that in people experiencing depression there is a change in their brain-messaging chemicals. These chemicals are important in regulating mood and various other important functions. When an imbalance of brain chemicals occurs, it is believed that depression can result, although it is also possible that the chemical change is the result of depression.[5]

Genetic

Some types of depression, like major depression, run in families, suggesting that some element of depression may be inherited, although there is no single depression gene. What exactly is inherited is not known but may include changes in brain structures or brain function, including alterations to the physiological responses to stress.[6]

Hormonal

Hormones are also chemical messages that communicate within the body as a whole and are thought to contribute to mood. Hormonal changes occur mainly in women due to menstrual cycle changes, pregnancy, miscarriage, post-natal period, pre-menopause and menopause.

Environment/background

Certain environmental causes such as family factors and adverse childhood experiences are considered to increase a person's chance of developing depression: for

RETHINK

example, poor parent–child relationship, marital discord and divorce, neglect, physical abuse and sexual abuse. Such experiences can lead to negative thought patterns and low self-esteem which can trigger depression later in life, particularly when combined with stressful events such as loss of a job or close relationship.[7]

Lifestyle

Food: There has been more attention in recent years to the effect that food and drink can have on our mental wellbeing. Certain foods contain 'essential fatty acids' which help keep the brain healthy and regulate mood. Other foods are known to have a detrimental effect on mood.[8]

Exercise: As well as being essential to your physical health, exercise regulates blood sugar, improves mood stability and releases mood-enhancing endorphins.[9] An exercise programme is now recommended by NICE as a treatment for mild to moderate depression.[10]

Substance misuse: Excessive substance use can affect the functioning of the brain and some research suggests this can have long-lasting results. Excessive alcohol consumption is thought to be linked with depression due to depleting essential fatty acids in the brain.[11]

Physical illness

Mood change and depression are more common in people suffering from physical illnesses than in people who are well. The link between physical illness and depression could be attributed to several factors, perhaps interacting with each other. People from poorer backgrounds are more prone to physical illness due to environmental factors, and mental illness due to increased stress. Negative reactions of others to people with physical illness (stigma) can cause depression. Those with depression may be more prone then to developing physical illness, and the reverse is also true, that physical illness can directly cause mental illness. It

is also more common amongst people with a number of forms of chronic illnesses, and so should be an important consideration in treatment plans.[12]

Medication and depression

There is a lot of disagreement in medical literature about the role of prescribed medications in inducing symptoms of depression. However, review of research has suggested that the following drugs may be associated with depression: Beta-blockers, Corticosteroids, Calcium channel blockers, Levodopa.

If depressive symptoms develop after taking a new medicine, then advice should be sought from a doctor about whether to try an alternative.[13]

References

1   Appleby L., Cooper J., Amos T., Faragher B. Psychological autopsy study of suicides by people aged under 35. *British Journal of Psychiatry* (1999) 175: 168-74.

2   Mental Health Foundation: http://www.mentalhealth.org.uk/information/mental-health-a-z/depression/

3   Royal College of Psychiatrists: www.rcpsych.ac.uk/mentalhealthforall/problems/postnatalmentalhealth

4   The National Institute of Mental Heath: http://www.nimh.nih.gov/health/publications/depression/complete-index.shtml#pub5

5   http://www.overcomedepression.co.uk/MajorDepression.html

6   Tsuang MT, Faraone SV. *The genetics of mood disorders.* Baltimore, MD: Johns Hopkins University Press, 1990.

7   The National Institute For Clinical Excellence: http://www.nice.org.uk/nicemedia/pdf/CG23fullguideline.pdf

8   The Mental Health Foundation: Dr. Deborah Cornah, Feeding Minds Report.

9   The Mental Health Foundation: Exercise and Depression.

10   The National Institute For Clinical Excellence: http://www.nice.org.uk/nicemedia/pdf/CG23fullguideline.pdf

11   Mathews-Larson, Joan: Alcohol – The bio-chemical connection.

12   Machale, Siobhan, Managing depression in physical illness, *Advances in Psychiatric Treatment* (2002) 8: 297-305.

13   Machale, Siobhan, Managing depression in physical illness, *Advances in Psychiatric Treatment* (2002) 8: 297-305.

14   The National Institute For Clinical Excellence: http://www.nice.org.uk/nicemedia/pdf/CG23fullguideline.pdf

15   The National Institute For Clinical Excellence: http://www.nice.org.uk/nicemedia/pdf/CG23fullguideline.pdf

16   IBID

17   IBID

Last updated January 2010

⇨ The above information is reprinted with kind permission from Rethink. To see the full version of this factsheet, and to see further factsheets about mental illness, please visit www.mentalhealthshop.org

RETHINK

Myths about depression quiz

Information from Boots WebMD.

1. Depression is harmful but not a major medical condition.
- ☐ Fact
- ☐ Myth

2. If a parent and grandparent had depression, you're bound to get it eventually.
- ☐ Fact
- ☐ Myth

3. Only emotionally troubled people become depressed.
- ☐ Fact
- ☐ Myth

4. Most people with depression never go to a mental health professional.
- ☐ Fact
- ☐ Myth

5. Depression is most common in elderly people.
- ☐ Fact
- ☐ Myth

6. Depression causes physical pain.
- ☐ Fact
- ☐ Myth

7. Talking about depression only makes it worse.
- ☐ Fact
- ☐ Myth

8. Being optimistic can cure depression.
- ☐ Fact
- ☐ Myth

Answers

1. Depression is harmful but not a major medical condition.

The correct answer is: myth

Depression isn't simply a temporary case of 'the blues'. It's a common, serious medical condition that can disrupt your daily life. At the extreme, people with depression may harm themselves. Brain imaging research shows that the brains of people with depression function differently than those of non-depressed people. In depressed people, brain areas that regulate mood, behaviour, thinking, appetite and sleep seem to function abnormally. Also, important brain chemicals called neurotransmitters appear to be out of balance.

2. If a parent and grandparent had depression, you're bound to get it eventually.

The correct answer is: myth

Because depression can run in families, scientists suspect that genes play a role. You're three times more likely to develop depression if your parents suffered depression, but it's not inevitable that you'll get the illness, too. Scientists believe the risk of developing depression results from a combination of genetic, biochemical, psychological and environmental factors.

3. Only emotionally troubled people become depressed.

The correct answer is: myth

Depression affects people from all walks of life, not just people with previous emotional troubles. Depression can develop after the loss of a loved one, trauma or other stressful situations like the loss of a job.

4. Most people with depression never go to a mental health professional.

The correct answer is: fact

The mental health charity SANE says most people with depression are treated by their GP, with only a small minority referred to a mental health specialist. Also, many depressed patients remain undiagnosed or undertreated. Some cases of depression are hard to treat. But the vast majority of cases are highly treatable with antidepressants and 'talking therapy' (psychotherapy) or cognitive behavioural therapy. The earlier treatment begins, the more effective it is.

5. Depression is most common in elderly people.

The correct answer is: myth

People assume the elderly suffer depression most often. In fact, middle-aged people aged 40 to 59 have the highest

rates of depression. Depression is not a normal part of ageing. However, ill health, medication side effects, social isolation and financial troubles can trigger depression in elderly people. Older people belong to a generation that often feels ashamed to admit to feelings of sadness and grief, but it's crucial that they seek help, especially because suicide is common in the elderly.

6. Depression causes physical pain.

The correct answer is: fact

Depression causes emotional symptoms such as anxiety, irritability and hopelessness, but it can also cause physical symptoms such as chest pain, queasy or nauseated sensations, dizziness or light-headedness, sleep problems, exhaustion, and changes in weight and appetite. It can also worsen back and joint pain and muscle aches.

7. Talking about depression only makes it worse.

The correct answer is: myth

Different types of psychotherapy, or talking therapy, have been proven effective in treating depression. For example, cognitive behavioural therapy (CBT) teaches people new ways of thinking to replace negative thoughts and behaviours that contribute to depression. In another approach, interpersonal therapy (IPT) helps people to understand troubled relationships and find ways to work through the difficulties.

8. Being optimistic can cure depression.

The correct answer is: myth

Depression can be debilitating. Most people with the disorder will require treatment to get better. Few can will themselves to get well through positive thinking. People with depression may need medication to help normalise brain chemicals.

Reviewed by Dr Rob Hicks on 1 June 2009

Sources

⇨ National Institute of Mental Health: 'Depression'.

⇨ American Psychiatric Association: 'Psychiatric News: Children of Depressed Parents Have More Health Problems'.

⇨ CDC: 'Depression in the United States Household Population, 2005-2006'.

⇨ MedlinePlus: 'Depression'.

⇨ WebMD Medical Reference: 'Depression: Recognizing the Physical Symptoms'.

⇨ Office for National Statistics – UK suicide rates.

⇨ SANE – Depression.

⇨ Reproduced with permission from Boots WebMD. Visit www.webmd.boots.com for more information.

Depression affects three out of four in UK

75% of people in the UK suffer from depression at some time in their lives, but only a third seek help, research has found.

The research found that depression is most commonly linked to money, with male sufferers likely to blame the recession for their condition.

Over half of people surveyed said they had felt down over money during the last year.

Depression is most commonly linked to money

The poll found that women sufferers are more worried about family or relationships, while January was seen as the most depressing month of the year due to post-Christmas credit card bills and cold weather.

Even mild depression needs to be identified and treated early, said Zelda Peters, director for mental health at the charity Turning Point.

'If it is not, the condition can worsen and lead to unemployment or long-term sickness, as well as negative behaviours such as drinking more, missing work or college and lying to family and friends.

'Anti-depressants are sometimes the answer but a huge range of treatments are also on offer, such as psychological therapies, which provide effective long-term relief.'

1 February 2010

⇨ The above information is reprinted with kind permission from *Nursing Times*. Visit www.nursingtimes.net for more information.

BOOTS WEBMD / NURSING TIMES

Seasonal Affective Disorder (SAD) or winter depression

Information from Depression Alliance Scotland.

What is SAD?

Seasonal Affective Disorder or SAD is a form of depression which develops in the autumn and improves in the spring. It is thought to be caused by lack of light in winter.

Who is affected by SAD?

Many people, whether or not they have SAD, find they dislike the dark mornings and early evenings of autumn and winter, preferring the longer outside light of the other seasons. However, seven per cent of people in Scotland will develop full blown SAD and a further 15 per cent of us will have the winter blues – a milder version.

Symptoms

People affected by SAD may experience the following:

⇨ Feeling low, depressed, feelings of despair, misery, guilt and anxiety.

⇨ Sleep problems – oversleeping but not waking up feeling refreshed, not being able to get out of bed, needing a nap in the afternoon, always feeling tired.

⇨ Overeating and food cravings – while it is common for people with other types of depression to not want to eat, people with SAD often crave sweet and starchy foods and may gain weight over the winter months.

⇨ Social problems – avoiding company, feeling irritable, a loss of libido.

⇨ Lethargy – feeling too tired to cope, everything seeming a huge effort, can't be bothered to do anything.

⇨ Physical symptoms – often joint pain or stomach problems, or a lowered resistance to infection.

Treating SAD

Light therapy

As SAD is caused by lack of light, recent research indicates that concentrating on increasing light exposure by artificial means is able to reduce the effects of SAD. This involves exposure to very bright light which must be at least 2500 lux. Lights used in offices and the home are around 200–500 lux so a special light box is needed. For many people sitting in front of a light box, allowing the light to reach the eyes, will alleviate most symptoms. You can buy or hire light boxes which emit the correct amount of light from various companies.

When using a light box you do not have to stare at the light, but get on with normal tasks like watching TV, reading, knitting, sewing, using the computer. The length of time you will need to sit in front of the light box depends on the brightness of the light you obtain. Treatment time usually varies from between 20 minutes and around one or two hours but manufacturers will normally advise you as to the optimal use of the equipment. If you are really busy and don't have time to sit in front of a box, some companies sell light visors which can be worn on the head while you do other things.

It is normally recommended that you start light treatment in early autumn, September or October and continue it until the days become lighter in March or April.

There are no absolute contra-indications for using a light box. This means that there are no medical conditions

or treatments that mean you absolutely shouldn't use a light box. However, because light boxes are very bright there are some risk factors. These include:

⇨ eye disease;

⇨ diabetes – which can cause problems in the eyes;

⇨ certain medication can make you more photo-sensitive.

Check with your doctor before starting light therapy to make sure that you are not at risk.

Getting out in the sun

Increasing exposure to sunlight is one way you can help to reduce symptoms. If you can afford a winter holiday in the sun, where you will obtain good sunlight but not excessive heat, this can be really helpful. Going skiing or to a snowy area can also help. If you can't afford to go abroad, it may help to get outside as often as possible, particularly at noon, which is the brightest part of the day.

Exercise

If you are also able to take part in regular physical exercise, such as swimming or walking, you may also find your symptoms of SAD getting better.

7% of people in Scotland will develop full blown SAD and a further 15% of us will have the winter blues – a milder version

Antidepressants

Because SAD is thought to be caused by disturbances in the brain chemical serotonin, newer antidepressants such as Prozac and Lustral, which act on serotonin, may help those affected by SAD. These can be used with light therapy. For more information on antidepressants, visit the antidepressants page on our website: www.dascot.org/depression/treatment/antidepressants.html

Other treatment

Other forms of treatment for depression like psycho-therapy, Cognitive Behaviour Therapy, nutrition and alternative remedies may be useful for people with SAD. Visit the treatment page of our website for more information: www.dascot.org/depression/treatment

Summer depression

Some people find that they have summer depression or 'Reverse Seasonal Affective Disorder'. They feel fine in the winter but experience symptoms in the summer.

According to one article, the condition affects an estimated 600,000 people in the UK. Summer depression is more likely to occur in hotter areas so it may not affect many people in Scotland.

Symptoms include insomnia, decreased appetite, weight loss, and agitation or anxiety. As in all depression, those affected by summer depression may feel miserable and low for no reason. There has been little research into summer depression and there is clearly a need for more investigation into this topic.

Also, in particularly overcast Scottish summers where there is not much sun, those affected by winter SAD may experience symptoms. Using a light box in the summer may help.

⇨ The above information is reprinted with kind permission from Depression Alliance Scotland. Visit www.dascot.org for more information.

© Depression Alliance Scotland

Statistics on mental health

Information from the Mental Health Foundation.

⇨ One in four people will experience some kind of mental health problem in the course of a year.

⇨ Mixed anxiety and depression is the most common mental disorder in Britain.

⇨ Women are more likely to have been treated for a mental health problem than men.

⇨ About 10% of children have a mental health problem at any one time.

⇨ Depression affects one in five older people living in the community and two in five living in care homes.

⇨ British men are three times as likely as British women to die by suicide.

⇨ The UK has one of the highest rates of self-harm in Europe, at 400 per 100,000 population.

⇨ Only one in ten prisoners has no mental disorder.

⇨ The above information is reprinted with kind permission from the Mental Health Foundation. Visit www.mentalhealth.org.uk for more information.

© Mental Health Foundation

DEPRESSION ALLIANCE SCOTLAND / MENTAL HEALTH FOUNDATION

Bipolar as a condition

Frequently asked questions.

How do I know if I have bipolar?

If you think you might have bipolar disorder, seek your GP's advice. If necessary, your GP will refer you to a specialist – usually a psychiatrist. Diagnosis should always be undertaken by an appropriately trained healthcare professional. It is not advisable to self-diagnose.

Often psychiatrists will use guidelines to make a diagnosis. These guidelines set out the symptoms that have to be present to make a firm diagnosis.

The psychiatrist will ask questions about your family history and background to see if other people in your family may have had the condition. S/he may also take notes of your age, when you first experienced the symptoms and details of the exact symptoms you have had before making a diagnosis. All this information helps to make decisions about your treatment.

Is there a medical test for bipolar?

Not as such. Although you should always seek professional opinion and advice, there is an MDF self-assessment tool available that you can use as a starting point in discussions with your health care providers – http://www.mdf.org.uk/?o=56890

On average it can take an individual experiencing bipolar disorder ten years to get a correct diagnosis. This screening questionnaire was developed by Dr Ronald Pies to help lead to an accurate diagnosis earlier than might otherwise be the case. It is applicable to the entire spectrum of bipolar disorders.

As with any assessment tool, it is not intended as a substitute for professional opinion and advice.

What are the symptoms of bipolar disorder? I have 'ups' and 'downs' – do I have bipolar?

The main symptoms of bipolar disorder are mood swings from extremely happy (mania) to extremely sad (depression). The periods of mania and depression can be extreme and without treatment often interfere with everyday life.

Mania (high)

If you are having a manic episode, you often cannot tell that anything is wrong. It can seem like other people are being critical, negative or unhelpful. You feel full of energy and enthusiasm and might feel that you do not need to sleep and are active all the time. You may make rush decisions on the spur of the moment that can have disastrous consequences.

Common symptoms:

⇨ Incoherent, rapid or disjointed thinking.

⇨ Talkative.

⇨ Severely impaired judgement.

⇨ Ever-changing plans and ideas.

⇨ Constant elation and/or euphoria.

⇨ Inappropriate optimism.

⇨ Grandiose delusions or ideas.

⇨ Gross over-estimation of personal capability.

⇨ Waking early and highly energised.

⇨ Need for little sleep (less than five hours).

⇨ Promiscuous/increased sexual behaviour.

⇨ Buying and spending freely, beyond financial means.

⇨ Verbal aggression towards partner, relatives and friends.

A sense of identity and self can be distorted by the illness. Sometimes the term 'psychosis' (losing touch with reality) is used to describe these symptoms when they are severe.

It is important to remember that these are only some of the more common symptoms of mania and not everybody will experience them all.

Depression (low)

Most people who have a diagnosis of bipolar illness will usually experience depression at some time. This will often follow an episode of mania where the trauma of the manic episode can sometimes compound the depression. (For some people depression will be more likely to occur in winter months.)

Depression is far more than the feeling of being fed up and miserable that everyone experiences. You feel useless, desperate, guilty, hopeless and unable to think properly. You may find it difficult, if not impossible, to do the ordinary things of everyday life.

Common symptoms:

⇨ Feeling of emptiness or worthlessness (as opposed to sadness).

⇨ Loss of energy and motivation for many or all everyday activities, including washing, feeding and caring for oneself.

⇨ Pessimism and negativity about most things or everything.

⇨ Loss of concentration.

⇨ Loss of perspective.

⇨ Loss of sense of self.

⇨ Self-doubt and self-blame.

⇨ Isolation from friends and family.

⇨ Poor quality of sleep, with early morning waking.

⇨ Inability to get out of bed until late morning or early afternoon.

Thoughts of death and/or planning suicide can be common, but may be difficult to discuss.

During both the manic and depressive periods of the illness it is possible that some people will experience strange sensations such as seeing, hearing, smelling or tasting things that are not there (hallucinations). Or you might believe things that seem irrational to other people (delusions). This is called psychosis or a psychotic episode.

The main symptoms of bipolar disorder are mood swings from extremely happy (mania) to extremely sad (depression)

Once again, it is important to remember that these are only some of the more common symptoms of depression and not everybody will experience all of them.

What causes bipolar disorder?

The exact cause of bipolar disorder is not fully understood. It does seem to run in families, which suggests that genetics are involved. Around 10–15 per cent of the nearest relatives of people with bipolar disorder also have a mood disorder.

It is also known that very stressful life events and physical illness can trigger periods of the illness. The causes are, therefore, far from simple to establish.

Are there different types of bipolar disorder?

Yes, there are different conditions that fall under the category of bipolar disorder.

Some mental health professionals consider that bipolar is more a group of different mood disorders rather than one specific diagnosis. They refer instead to the 'bipolar spectrum'.

Bipolar (Manic Depression):

Bipolar is a serious mental health problem involving extreme swings of mood (highs and lows). It is also known as manic depression. Both men and women, of any age from adolescence onwards and from any social or ethnic background, can develop bipolar. It often first occurs when work, study, family or emotional pressures are at their greatest. In women it can also be triggered by childbirth or during the menopause.

Hypomania:

Often explained as a less severe form of mania, someone experiencing hypomania may seem very self-confident and euphoric but may react with sudden anger, impatience or become irritable – sometimes for the slightest reason. S/he may have more ideas than usual, be unusually busy, work too much or be very creative, but not be able to focus on anything for long or switch off and relax. S/he may become more reckless than usual, which might mean errors of judgement at work or in relationships, or be more talkative or challenging with people.

Schizoaffective Disorder:

This relatively rare disorder is defined as 'the presence of psychotic symptoms in the absence of mood changes for at least two weeks in a patient who has a mood disorder.' The diagnosis is used when an individual does not fit diagnostic standards for either schizophrenia or 'affective' (mood) disorders such as depression and bipolar.

Some people may have symptoms of both a depressive disorder and schizophrenia at the same time, or they may have symptoms of schizophrenia without mood symptoms.

Cyclothymia:

Cyclothymia is a mood disorder in which the person displays the characteristic ups and downs (depressions and euphorias) of bipolar to a much lower extent, to the point of not qualifying for a diagnosis of bipolar. These symptoms must last for a period of at least two years, with no period longer than two months in which they have been at a normal state, and no mixed episodes may have occurred.

'Mixed' state:

Symptoms of mania and depression are present at the same time, which may result in agitation, trouble sleeping, significant change in appetite, psychosis and suicidal thoughts.

Psychosis:

Sometimes severe mania or depression is accompanied by periods of psychosis. Psychotic symptoms include hallucinations and delusions. Psychotic symptoms associated with bipolar typically reflect the extreme mood state at the time (e.g. grandiosity during mania, worthlessness during depression).

MDF

Rapid cycling:

This is defined as four or more episodes within a 12-month period. This type of bipolar tends to be more resistant to treatment than non-rapid-cycling bipolar. Children and young people may be more prone to rapid cycling than adults.

Euphoric mania: person is elated and full of optimism.

Dysphoric mania: person is high but also irritable, impatient, agitated.

Euthymia: stable mood.

Unipolar depression: major depressive disorder, with no mania.

Dysthymia: less severe depression than unipolar depression, but can be more persistent.

What is the difference between unipolar depression and bipolar?

Bipolar depression is the depressive phase of bipolar. It may alternate with mania or hypomania. It can also occur at the same time as mania in a mixed episode.

There is one set of symptoms for depressive episodes. These may occur in bipolar or major depressive disorder (unipolar depression). Each person's experience is a little bit different. Researchers have studied possible differences in symptoms of bipolar and unipolar depression.

With bipolar depression, people are more likely to have symptoms like feelings of worthlessness and loss of interest. They may also have increased sleep and appetite, and feel slowed down. There might be psychotic symptoms such as delusions or hallucinations. Bipolar depression is thought to have a higher risk of suicidal thoughts and attempts. Unipolar depression is more likely to include anxiety, tearfulness, insomnia and loss

of appetite. It is not always easy for the person who has depressive symptoms to identify and describe them.

More than half of people with bipolar experience depression before they experience mania. Doctors often recommend starting treatment with a mood stabiliser instead of an antidepressant if a person might have bipolar disorder.

What treatment is available?

There are a number of different treatments for bipolar.

Medication

There are various forms of medication offered to people with bipolar, including mood stabilisers, antipsychotics, antidepressants. Medication varies from one individual to another, and medications should only be taken under professional medical advice.

Medicines which are taken long term are often called mood stabilisers. These drugs are used both to treat mania as well as to prevent further episodes of mania and depression. They reduce the extreme changes of mood and activity that are responsible for the disturbances in sleep, appetite, thought processes, judgement and sexual activity that occur in manic depression. It is generally preferable to take these medications on a continuous rather than 'stop-start' basis.

Antipsychotics

Antipsychotic drugs appear to act chiefly by blocking some dopamine receptors, but also affect other chemicals in the brain. They are used to calm and stabilise during an acute manic episode. On occasions, antipsychotic drugs are taken on a long-term basis to help stabilise an individual and reduce the incidence of psychotic episodes. If you require an antipsychotic, you should consider the newer 'atypical' antipsychotics as a first choice as they are generally better tolerated and appear less likely to cause movement disorders (extrapyramidal or Parkinsonian side-effects).

Antidepressants

These include:

Selective Serotonin Re-uptake Inhibitors (SSRIs), the most well known of this group being fluoxetine (Prozac) and paroxetine (Seroxat). SSRIs increase the concentration of the chemical neurotransmitter serotonin at the nerve endings in the brain. The level of serotonin in the brain affects mood. If stopped suddenly, there can be withdrawal symptoms.

SSRI-related antidepressants are new antidepressants that are similar to SSRIs, but in addition they may increase the level of noradrenaline within the brain. Their side effects are similar to other antidepressants but, as with all new drugs, their full effects may not yet be known.

Tricyclic antidepressants (TCAs) are well established but may carry a greater risk of precipitating a switch into mania than the SSRIs. They also have a high incidence of side effects, which may further limit their use.

Monoamine oxidase inhibitors (MAOIs) are not often prescribed because they interact with a wide range of food, alcoholic drinks and drugs that contain tyramine. Cheese, broad beans, OXO, Marmite and other yeast-based products, as well as pickled herrings, other preserved foods, lager beers and wine all interact with MAOIs.

Talking therapies

There are a number of talking therapies available from the NHS, including counselling, cognitive-behaviour therapy and psychoanalytic or psychodynamic psychotherapy.

Most of us want somebody to talk to, who listens and accepts us, especially when we are going through a bad time. Sometimes it can be easier to talk to a stranger than to relatives or friends. Therapists are trained to listen and to help you find your own answers, without judging you.

Some therapists will aim to find the root cause of your problem and help you deal with this, some will help you change your behaviour or negative thoughts, while others simply aim to support you.

Self-Management Training

Self-Management Training is designed to give people diagnosed with bipolar a thorough and comprehensive understanding of the concepts, tools and techniques involved in learning to self-manage extreme mood swings.

Research has shown that learning to self-manage bipolar is an invaluable part of stabilising the condition. It can significantly improve an individual's affective perception of areas such as self-esteem and reduction in suicidal thoughts.

Complementary therapies

Some people with bipolar use complementary therapies to ease their symptoms. There are many different complementary therapies, including: aromatherapy, anthroposophy, Ayurvedic medicine, Bach Flower Remedies, exercise, movement and relaxation, healing and touch therapies, herbal medicine (Western), homeopathy, hypnotherapy, massage, naturopathy, nutritional therapy, reflexology, traditional Chinese medicine, transcendental meditation and yoga.

Electroconvulsive Therapy

ECT has been used for more than 50 years, yet it remains highly controversial. There remains a great deal of public concern about ECT's continued use, yet it is a safe and effective treatment for severe depression. It provides a welcome relief from the suffering caused by a severe depression for many patients.

What powers do my family have?

Under the Mental Health Act (1983) you have a 'nearest relative' who will be involved in decisions about whether you will be detained. You do not get to choose your nearest relative. They must be related to you in a way that is described in the Mental Health Act (1983). Your nearest relative may change over time as your situation changes.

If you or your nearest relative are unhappy about them taking on this role, you can write a letter naming someone else to act as your nearest relative. They should tell at least one of your doctors or other people responsible for your care. The nearest relative can also change their mind at any time about whether someone else should take on this role, but they need to do this in writing.

What can my nearest relative do for me?

They have several powers and responsibilities:

They can apply for you to be admitted to hospital.

The approved social worker must tell the nearest relative if they have applied (or are applying) for you to be detained under section 2 of the Mental Health Act (1983).

The approved social worker must talk to the nearest relative if they plan to detain you under section 3 (unless it is not practical to do this, or it would cause an unreasonable delay). Your nearest relative can object to the application to detain you. However, the approved social worker can ask the court to appoint someone else as your nearest relative if the objection is unreasonable.

They can apply for you to be discharged from hospital, although the doctor in charge of the treatment can stop this.

Is having bipolar genetic?

Bipolar disorder has a strong genetic basis as a 'physical disorder' such as diabetes. Unfortunately, the genes involved in susceptibility, and hence likely to be of value in developing treatments, remain unidentified. Further medical research is being carried out.

The blessing and the curse – almost certainly the genes which in one combination can give rise to severe disabling bipolar illness, can in other combinations have advantages – 'the bipolar advantage'. This may explain why some exceptionally creative and successful people have relatives with bipolar disorder, severe depression and suicide in their family. It also explains why many people with bipolar disorder are gifted.

Source: http://www.bipolar-foundation.org

⇨ Information from MDF, the bipolar organisation. Visit www.mdf.org.uk for more.

© MDF

MDF

Same genes suspected in both depression and bipolar illness

Increased risk may stem from variation in gene on/off switch.

Researchers, for the first time, have pinpointed a genetic hotspot that confers risk for both bipolar disorder and depression. People with either of these mood disorders were significantly more likely to have risk versions of genes at this site than healthy controls. One of the genes, which codes for part of a cell's machinery that tells genes when to turn on and off, was also found to be over-expressed in the executive hub of bipolar patients' brains, making it a prime suspect. The results add to mounting evidence that major mental disorders overlap at the molecular level.

Major mood disorders affect 20 per cent of the population and are among the leading causes of disability worldwide

'People who carry the risk versions may differ in some dimension of brain development that may increase risk for mood disorders later in life,' explained Francis McMahon MD, of the NIMH Mood and Anxiety Disorders Program, who led the study.

McMahon and an international team of investigators, supported, in part by NIMH, report on the findings of their genome-wide meta-analysis online January 17, 2010 in the journal *Nature Genetics*.

Background

Major mood disorders affect 20 per cent of the population and are among the leading causes of disability worldwide. It's long been known that bipolar disorder and unipolar depression often run together in the same families, hinting at some shared lineage. Yet, until now, no common genes or chromosomal locations had been identified.

McMahon and colleagues analysed data from five different genome-wide association studies (GWAS) totalling more than 13,600 people, and confirmed their results in three additional independent samples totalling 4,677 people.

Findings of this study

Genetic variations on Chromosome 3 were significantly associated with both mood disorders. The suspect gene, called PBRM1, codes for a protein critical for chromatin remodelling, a key process in regulating gene expression. A neighbouring gene is involved in the proliferation of brain stem cells.

The researchers pinpointed a 'protective' version of the PBRM1 gene that is carried by 41 per cent of healthy controls, but only 38 per cent of people with bipolar and unipolar depression. The risk version was found in 62 per cent of mood disorder cases and 59 per cent of controls. The researchers also showed that PBRM1 is expressed more in the prefrontal cortex of people with bipolar disorder than in controls.

Significance

Since mood disorders likely involve altered gene expression during brain development and in response

to stress, PBRM1's profile makes it a good potential candidate gene. This first genetic evidence of unipolar/bipolar overlap is also the first significant genome-wide association with any psychiatric illness in the Chromosome 3p region.

However, the findings underscore limitations of the GWAS approach, which looks for connections to gene versions that are common in the population. Having one copy of this risk variant increases vulnerability for developing a mood disorder by a modest 15 per cent. Why do some people with this variant – and presumably other, yet to be discovered, shared risk genes – develop bipolar disorder while others develop unipolar depression or remain healthy? Environmental influences and epigenetic factors may be involved, suggest the researchers, who note that 'genetic association findings so far seem to account for little of the inherited risk for mood disorders'.

'Our results support the growing view that there aren't common genes with large effects that confer increased risk for mood disorders,' said McMahon. 'If there were, in this largest sample to date, we would have found them. The disorders likely involve many genes with small effects – and different genes in different families –

complicating the search. Rarer genes with large effects may also exist.'

What's next?

Ultimately, findings such as these may lead to identification of common biological pathways that may play a role in both unipolar and bipolar illness and suggest strategies for better treatment, said McMahon. The results add to other evidence of overlap that is spurring a new NIMH initiative to make sense of research findings that don't fit neatly into current diagnostic categories. See: *Genes and Circuitry, Not Just Clinical Observation, to Guide Classification for Research*.

Citation: Meta-analysis of genome-wide association data identifies a risk locus for major mood disorders on 3p21.1.the Bipolar Disorder Genome Study (BiGS) Consortium, McMahon FJ, Akula N, Schulze TG, Muglia P, Tozzi F, Detera-Wadleigh SD, Steele CJ, Breuer R, Strohmaier J, Wendland JR, Mattheisen M, Mühleisen TW, Maier W, Nöthen MM, Cichon S, Farmer A, Vincent JB, Holsboer F, Preisig M, Rietschel M. Nat Genet. 2010 Jan 17. PMID: 20081856

28 January 2010

⇨ Information from the National Institute of Mental Health. Visit www.nimh.nih.gov for more information.

Depression linked to desire for fame, say scientists

People who suffer from depression and mania are more likely to focus on success, money and fame than others, research has found.

By Ben Leach

The study, published in the *British Journal of Clinical Psychology*, found that mania and depression may drive people to set higher goals.

Dr Johnson, one of the researchers from the University of California, Berkeley who conducted the study, said: 'Manic episodes are characterised by elevated mood as well as increased talkativeness, racing thoughts, decreased need for sleep and extreme distractibility.

'Mania has already been linked to a belief in the importance of achievement and so we wanted to discover whether it is also linked with higher expectations for the future.'

The research looked at the manic and depressive levels of 103 people, including 27 people with diagnosed manic depression – also known as bipolar disorder.

The subjects answered questionnaires designed to assess their ambitions, such as a desire for fame, material success or recognition.

Participants rated the likelihood of various things happening to them, such as: 'You will appear regularly on TV', 'You will have 20 million dollars or more'.

The study concluded that the people who had experienced episodes of mania during their lives had the highest expectations of achieving popular success and financial success.

Dr Johnson said: 'This pattern suggests that people with manic or bipolar tendencies are drawn to focus on success, money and popular fame.

'These results suggest that mania, along with all of its costs, may also drive people to set higher goals. In some cases they achieve them, giving us a glimpse into the advantages that can accompany this highly painful disorder.'

Last week a study found that insomnia and other sleep-related problems could lead to depression as well as other psychiatric conditions.

Sleep problems, while long linked to mental health conditions, were thought to be a side-effect. But scientists at Harvard University in America found that sleeping difficulties could cause some mental health problems.

2 March 2009

NATIONAL INSTITUTE OF MENTAL HEALTH / THE TELEGRAPH

Post-natal depression

You have a beautiful new baby, you've recovered well from the birth, but you feel low, you can't sleep, and find yourself crying for no reason at all.

It's understandable: you're physically and emotionally exhausted, after all, and getting to grips with the reality of looking after a baby. But some mums – anything from one in ten to around half, depending on which survey you read – have the more serious problem of post-natal depression, or PND.

This isn't the same as the 'baby blues', which the majority of mums experience in the first few days after the birth, often coinciding with the day their milk comes in.

⇨ Post-natal depression starts in the first weeks or months of a baby's life, and lasts much longer than the baby blues.

⇨ Symptoms include exhaustion, loneliness and isolation, low energy levels, extreme mood swings, sadness, aggression, irrationality, being neurotic, feeling anxious, and even thoughts of or actual self-harm or harming the baby.

⇨ You may feel overwhelmed by everyday tasks, and some mums find it difficult to bond with their baby.

Elaine A Hanzak, a leading authority on postnatal depression (www.hanzak.com), says: 'Often mums suffer needlessly because they think their low mood and difficulty in functioning after the arrival of a baby are "normal". Do not ignore it. There is no need to feel ashamed about it, it is not a sign of weakness, and you are not a bad mother. You are unwell.'

If you suspect you are suffering from PND, talk to your GP or health visitor as soon as you can. There is lots of help and support available, including medication, counselling, support groups, or self-help methods.

Mum-of-one Bernadette says: 'I could remember how I felt before the baby was born so knew that I wasn't right. A last-straw scenario finally forced me to make an appointment with my GP and then it was straightforward to get help. If only I had realised earlier that I only had to ask for it.'

> ***Some mums – anything from one in ten to around half, depending on which survey you read – have the more serious problem of post-natal depression, or PND***

It is often those close to the mother who notice something is not quite right. Dads should look out for:

⇨ extreme changes in behaviour;

⇨ obsessive habits such as checking the baby repeatedly;

⇨ not wanting others to hold or take the baby;

⇨ extreme tearfulness, expressing feelings of being a failure, or not wanting to leave the house or get out of bed.

Mum-of-two Maddy, who was diagnosed with PND when her first child was seven months old, says: 'My partner noticed before I did that something was wrong – I didn't actually feel depressed. But I had slowly become more and more anxious and angry, and was obsessive about my daughter's routine. After I hugely overreacted to something at a family dinner, my partner called my health visitor and GP. I just wish I'd acknowledged earlier that something wasn't right.'

If you are a dad and suspect your partner is showing signs of PND:

⇨ Offer plenty of emotional and practical support.

⇨ Find out more about the condition and encourage your partner to talk to health professionals.

Likelihood of going to GP for help about a mental health problem.

Legend: Very likely, Quite likely, Neither likely nor unlikely, Quite unlikely, Very unlikely, Don't know

	All	Age 16-34	Age 35-54	Age 55+
Very likely	53%	47%	53%	59%
Quite likely	27%	30%	26%	26%
Neither likely nor unlikely	6%	7%	8%	4%
Quite unlikely	6%	7%	7%	5%
Very unlikely	4%	6%	7% (2%)	3%
Don't know	3%	3%	4%	3%

Source: Attitudes to mental illness 2009 Research Report, May 2009. TNS UK for the Care Services Improvement Partnership, Department of Health (crown copyright).

BOUNTY

⇨ Don't take it personally or accuse her of being lazy: she is ill and needs help to get better.

There are many possible causes of PND, including:

⇨ hormonal changes;

⇨ a family or personal history of depression;

⇨ traumatic birth experience;

⇨ stresses in the last three months of pregnancy such as bereavement, moving house, marital or family conflicts.

So is there anything you can do to avoid it?

Elaine Hanzak suggests the best thing you can do is be kind to yourself: 'We put great pressures on new mothers to be slim, active and possibly working again within months of giving birth, with a perfect home and content child. This simply isn't the reality and we set ourselves up for feelings of failure.' Try these tips to help you cope.

If you have a history of mental health problems or have suffered PND with a previous baby, seek help before the birth and put plans in place for maximum support in the early weeks to ease your worries.

Postnatal depression counsellor Lisa Tanner adds: 'Please don't suffer in silence. Ask for help as soon as possible, as the sooner PND is detected, the sooner it can be treated.'

Above all, remember that it is not your fault, you are not alone and you will get better.

Where to get help:

⇨ Speak to your health visitor and/or GP first.

⇨ The Association for Post-Natal Illness (APNI): http://apni.org or call 020 7386 0868.

⇨ There are also many books and websites for information and support, including Elaine Hanzak's *Eyes Without Sparkle – a journey through postnatal illness.* (Radcliffe, 2005).

⇨ www.mothersvoice.org.uk offers support and information to anyone affected by post-natal depression. You can chat online anonymously.

Puerperal psychosis

This is the most extreme form of mental illness after the birth of a baby. It's very rare, affecting just one in 500 newly-delivered mums. Symptoms include hallucinations, agitation, confusion and even urges to harm yourself or your baby. It is frightening for everyone involved, and it is important to get urgent medical help. For more information go to www.puerperalpsychosis.org.uk

⇨ The above information is reprinted with kind permission from Bounty. Visit www.bounty.com for more.

© Bounty

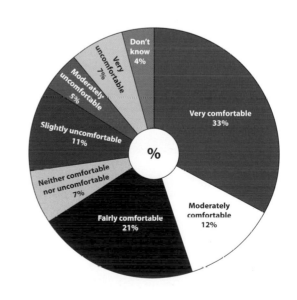

How comfortable would you feel talking to a friend or family member about your mental health?

- Don't know 4%
- Very uncomfortable 7%
- Moderately uncomfortable 5%
- Slightly uncomfortable 11%
- Neither comfortable nor uncomfortable 7%
- Fairly comfortable 21%
- Moderately comfortable 12%
- Very comfortable 33%

Source: Attitudes to mental illness 2009 Research Report, May 2009. TNS UK for the Care Services Improvement Partnership, Department of Health (crown copyright).

New dads get depressed too

Post-natal depression doesn't just affect mums.

By Nick Duerden

According to a series of recent books on fatherhood, it seems that fathers don't always experience the instantaneous love for their newborn child that we are so frequently told (wrongly) that mothers do. While I can't comment for every man out there, I can say that, personally, bonding with my daughter was one of the harder things I've had to do in adult life.

I simply had no idea how to prepare for such a monumental upheaval. Unlike my wife, I never quite felt the same sudden urge she did to start a family. I say sudden because, in the decade I'd known her, she had always told me she would never want children. But then, by her mid-30s, she began to experience what she could only describe as an increasingly overwhelming and biological need to have them. I rather went along with the whole thing hoping that, emotionally, I would catch up with her. (I did, though later rather than sooner.)

Pain

But all this shouldn't be so surprising, I think. How was I supposed to feel something positive for a new person who, just moments before she arrived into the world, had been causing all manner of pain to a woman I was mostly still quite fond of? My daughter emerged after the kind of labour that really did warrant the description 'hard', if only because it went on so long. And when she was finally presented to me by one of the midwives, I was confronted by a complete stranger, and a demanding one at that. She wanted only one thing after birth, and it wasn't me.

A newborn will never need its father as much as it does its mother, and all for good and obvious reasons. But this can make a man suddenly feel like a spare wheel, and he can even become a little resentful, if only because after a baby comes along the balance of power at home is promptly shattered. And who could get used to something like that overnight?

> *How was I supposed to feel something positive for a new person who, just moments before she arrived into the world, had been causing all manner of pain to a woman I was mostly still quite fond of?*

Research

Post-natal depression affects as many as one in 14 men. But in a society where post-natal depression in women has only recently been accepted, there's little research into it or acknowledgement of its existence. 'Fatherhood depression is an under-researched area,' says Professor Lorraine Sherr, Head of Health and Psychology at London's Royal Free Hospital. 'It isn't that fathers don't want to engage on the subject, just that people haven't really bothered targeting them.'

Will Courtenay, a psychotherapist and founder of PostpartumMen.com, a site for men experiencing post-partum depression, said recently that, '[Some men] can't stand to be around their baby, they can't stand the smell or the sound of their child screaming...'

Fear and exclusion of people with mental illness, by age.

Legend: Aged 16-34 | Aged 35-54 | Aged 55+

Downgrades neighbourhood
- Aged 16-34: 19%
- Aged 35-54: 19%
- Aged 55+: 25%

Foolish to marry
- Aged 16-34: 10%
- Aged 35-54: 12%
- Aged 55+: 18%

Excluded from public office
- Aged 16-34: 17%
- Aged 35-54: 17%
- Aged 55+: 31%

Should be hospitalised
- Aged 16-34: 24%
- Aged 35-54: 15%
- Aged 55+: 21%

% 0 5 10 15 20 25 30 35

Source: Attitudes to mental illness 2009 Research Report, May 2009. TNS UK for the Care Services Improvement Partnership, Department of Health (Crown copyright).

NICK DUERDEN

Hormones

He went on to suggest that shifting male hormones may play a role (men's testosterone levels drop by almost 50 per cent immediately after the birth of a child, effectively making us half the man we used to be), but a perhaps more significant factor is whether or not their partners themselves are depressed: 'Half of all men whose partners have post-partum depression are depressed themselves,' he said.

'Half of all men whose partners have post-partum depression are depressed themselves'

Michael Lewis, author of the book *Home Game: An Accidental Guide to Fatherhood*, recently admitted that a month after his daughter was born, 'I would have felt only an obligatory sadness had she been rolled over by a truck. Six months later, I'd have thrown myself in front of a truck to save her from harm. What transformed me from a monster into a father? I do not know.'

Helpless

As for myself, I became aware of a low-level kind of depression that haunted me for a few weeks after the birth, the longest of my life. I was immediately relegated to a bit part in my wife's life when I'd previously been leading man, and while mother and baby bonded, I reeled around the house wondering quite what my new role

entailed. I felt shut-out and helpless, confused, and with no idea what to do next. The baby had turned our universe upside down, and I struggled to find a toehold.

But crucially for me, my wife was adamant that we go through this as much together as possible, and that I be every bit as hands-on as her – because if I didn't, how else was I to bond with my daughter?

She was right. I found that the more I attended to all the crying, the nappies, the vomiting, the freak illnesses that departed as quickly as they had arrived (and often in the middle of the night), the more I felt a connection form. In other words, I began to get to know this little girl, and found I rather liked her.

Smile

The real turning point, though, came a few months in, when I began to think that perhaps she liked me, too. Being on the receiving end of what appeared to be a very deliberate smile prompted something inside me to open up, and all those previously bottled up feelings to come out in an excitable rush, and I felt myself perhaps belatedly capable of fatherhood at last.

What a relief – because before then, if I'm honest, it had often felt as if I could have gone either way.

24 November 2009

⇨ This article was written by Nick Duerden, the author of *The Reluctant Fathers' Club*, a memoir on fatherhood. It previously appeared on the ParentlinePlus website. Visit www.parentlineplus.org.uk for more information.

© *Nick Duerden*

NICK DUERDEN

Men and mental health: get it off your chest

⇨ **37% of men are feeling worried or low.**

⇨ **Middle-aged men are seven times more likely than women to have suicidal thoughts.**

⇨ **Only 23% of men would see their GP if they felt low for over a fortnight.**

⇨ **Men were only half as likely to talk to friends about problems as women.**

Leading mental health charity Mind today (Monday 11 May 2009) publishes the shocking new report *Men and mental health: Get it off your chest,* presenting evidence that the recession is having an adverse affect on men's mental health. Mind's YouGov survey found almost 40% of men are worried or low at the moment and the top three issues playing on their minds are job security, work and money. A small number of men were even experiencing suicidal thoughts – of these, middle-aged men were much more likely than women to have suicidal thoughts. Middle-aged men currently have the highest suicide rate in England and Wales.

Two-thirds of men under 35 years old were out of work when they took their own life

Mind's *Get it off your chest* campaign aims to get men to recognise the importance of talking about their problems and is calling for a strategy on men's mental health, to match the existing women's mental health strategy. Supporters with personal experience include Lord Melvyn Bragg, Alastair Campbell, Stephen Fry, actor Joe McGann and Heart FM DJ Matt Wilkinson.

Mind's new YouGov survey of over 2000 men and women found that:

⇨ 31% of men would feel embarrassed about seeking help for mental distress.

⇨ Just 14% of men (35–44 years old) would see a GP if they felt low compared to 37% of women.

⇨ 4% of young men (18–24 years old) would see a counsellor if they felt low compared to 13% of young women.

⇨ Only 31% of men would talk to their family about feeling low compared to nearly half of women.

⇨ Almost twice as many men as women get angry when they are worried.

⇨ 10% of men say they find sex the best way to relax compared to 4% of women.

⇨ Almost twice as many men as women drink alcohol to cope with feeling down.

⇨ Women are nearly five times more likely to get tearful than men.

⇨ 45% of men think they can fight off feeling down compared to 36% of women.

2.7 million men in England currently have a mental health problem like depression, anxiety or stress. Even though men and women experience mental health problems in roughly equal numbers, men are much less likely to be diagnosed and treated for it. The consequences of suffering in silence can be fatal – 75% of all suicides are by men. The recession could make the situation much worse, with one in seven men developing depression within six months of losing their jobs. Unemployment also increases the risk of suicide, with research showing that two-thirds of men under 35 years old were out of work when they took their own life.

Mental health problems impact certain groups of men in different ways. African Caribbean men are more likely to receive disproportionately aggressive treatment – they are three times more likely than white men to be formally detained under the Mental Health Act and are more likely to receive invasive medical treatments such as electroconvulsive therapy. Gay and bisexual men are at significantly higher risk too, being over four times more likely than heterosexual men to attempt suicide.

Mind's Chief Executive Paul Farmer said:

'The recession is clearly having a detrimental impact on the nation's mental health but men in particular are struggling with the emotional impact. Being a breadwinner is something that is still crucial to the male psyche, so if a man loses his job he loses a large part of his identity, putting his mental wellbeing in jeopardy. The problem is that too many men wrongly believe that admitting mental distress makes them weak and this kind of self-stigma can cost lives.

'At this time, it's really important that it's as easy as possible for men to find the help they need. The Government has encouraged Primary Care Trusts to use some £80m on mental health and the recession this year, and there's clearly a real need for them to act now to address men's needs.

'When men look for help, they can be put off by health premises that are geared more towards women. GP surgeries offering women's magazines can feel like a hairdressers and make men feel uncomfortable. The NHS must become more "male-friendly", offering treatments that appeal to men like exercise on prescription or computerised therapy and advertising their services in places men frequent.

'It is a major health inequality that a mental health strategy exists for women but not men. There is an urgent need for the Government to address this in the New Horizons strategy for mental health. At the heart of this is a need to help men to recognise the importance of talking about their problems and make it easier for them to ask for help.'

Stephen Fry said: 'For so long I tried to get on with my life and career, somehow coping with the huge highs and lows I experienced. If I had felt able to get it off my chest when I was younger I could have got more of the support I needed. Mind's campaign will hopefully encourage men to speak out more – stumbling through and hiding behind a front of bravado doesn't solve anything. Seek professional help when you need it – and support Mind to get better help and services out there.'

Alastair Campbell said: 'Many people, especially men, find it very hard to be open about mental fragility. They see it as a sign of weakness, and do not like to ask for help. Or they cover it with drink or drugs or behaviour generally likely to end in tears. I certainly support Mind's call for a Government-specific mental health strategy for men tailored to their needs. They have one for women and children so why not men?'

Mind's recommendations include:

⇨ The Government must produce the first men's mental health strategy.

⇨ The criteria for diagnosing mental health problems should be expanded to include male acting out behaviour (taking drugs, drinking, getting aggressive) as well as traditional signs of depression (sleepless nights, crying, feeling low).

⇨ Men should be offered 'male-friendly' treatments like computerised therapy or exercise.

⇨ Health services should be advertised in places men frequent, such as gyms, pubs or the workplace.

⇨ GP surgeries should be gender-neutral: men are often put off by what they consider an overly feminine environment.

⇨ Employers must do more to support their stressed male employees.

⇨ The needs of black and minority ethnic men must be made a priority for Strategic Health Authorities when the Delivering Race Equality strategy ends.

⇨ The relationship between sexuality, gender and mental wellbeing should be a core part of the training given to health and social services professionals.

11 May 2009

⇨ The above press release is reprinted with kind permission from Mind. Visit www.mind.org.uk for more.

© *Mind*

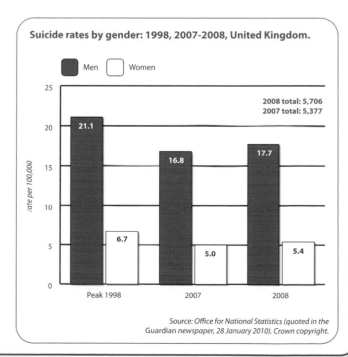

Suicide rates by gender: 1998, 2007-2008, United Kingdom.

Men   Women

rate per 100,000

2008 total: 5,706
2007 total: 5,377

Peak 1998: Men 21.1, Women 6.7
2007: Men 16.8, Women 5.0
2008: Men 17.7, Women 5.4

Source: Office for National Statistics (quoted in the Guardian newspaper, 28 January 2010). Crown copyright.

Depression as deadly as smoking but anxiety may be good for you

Information from the Institute of Psychiatry, King's College London.

A study by researchers at the University of Bergen, Norway, and the Institute of Psychiatry (IoP) at King's has found that depression is as much of a risk factor for mortality as smoking.

Utilising a unique link between a survey of over 60,000 people and a comprehensive mortality database, the researchers found that, over the four years following the survey, the mortality risk was increased to a similar extent in people who were depressed as in people who were smokers.

Dr Robert Stewart, who led the research team at the IoP, explains the possible reasons that may underlie these surprising findings: 'Unlike smoking, we don't know how causal the association with depression is but it does suggest that more attention should be paid to this link because the association persisted after adjusting for many other factors.'

The study also shows that patients with depression face an overall increased risk of mortality, while a combination of depression and anxiety in patients lowers mortality compared with depression alone. Dr Stewart explains: 'One of the main messages from this research is that "a little anxiety may be good for you".'

'It appears that we're talking about two risk groups here. People with very high levels of anxiety symptoms may be naturally more vulnerable due to stress, for example through the effects stress has on cardiovascular outcomes. On the other hand, people who score very low on anxiety measures, i.e. those who deny any symptoms at all, may be people who also tend not to seek help for physical conditions, or they may be people who tend to take risks. This would explain the higher mortality.'

In terms of the relationship between mortality and anxiety with depression as a risk factor, the research suggests that help-seeking behaviour may explain the pattern of outcomes. People with depression may not seek help or may fail to receive help when they do seek it, whereas the opposite may be true for people with anxiety.

Dr Stewart comments: 'It would certainly not surprise me at all to find that doctors are less likely to investigate physical symptoms in people with depression because they think that depression is the explanation, but may be more likely to investigate if someone is anxious because they think it will reassure them. These are conjectures but they would fit with the data.'

The researchers point out that the results should be considered in conjunction with other evidence suggesting a variety of adverse physical health outcomes and poor health associated with mental disorders such as depression and psychotic disorders.

In light of the findings, Dr Stewart makes suggestions on the focus of future developments in the treatment of depression and anxiety: 'The physical health of people with current or previous mental disorder needs a lot more attention than it gets at the moment.

'This applies to primary care, secondary mental health care and general hospital care in the sense that there should be more active screening for physical disorders and risk factors, such as blood pressure, cholesterol, adverse diet, smoking and lack of exercise, in people with mental disorders. This should be done in addition to more active treatment of disorders when present, and more effective general health promotion.'

Citation: 'Levels of anxiety and depression as predictors of mortality: the HUNT study'. *British Journal of Psychiatry* (2009) 195: 118-125. The full paper can be accessed here: http://bjp.rcpsych.org/cgi/content/abstract/195/2/118

17 November 2009

⇨ The above information is reprinted with kind permission from the Institute of Psychiatry, King's College London. Visit www.iop.kcl.ac.uk for more information.

© Institute of Psychiatry, King's College London

INSTITUTE OF PSYCHIATRY, KING'S COLLEGE LONDON

Depression and suicide

Information from Samaritans.

Overview

⇨ Depression is a very common mental health problem worldwide. It is estimated that it will become the second most common cause of disability, after heart disease, by 2020.

⇨ The term 'depression' covers a very wide range of experiences and level of illness forms, from mild to severe, transient to persistent.

⇨ A distinction should be made between 'unipolar' forms of depression such as major depression and dysthymia which involve persistent, low moods, and manic or 'bipolar' depression which involves bouts of low moods followed by extreme 'highs' or mania.

⇨ Unipolar forms of depression are more common in women than men. In Britain, 3–4% of men and 7–8% of women suffer from moderate to severe depression at any one time.

⇨ Bipolar depression affects men and women equally, and afflicts about five people in 1,000.

⇨ For people with severe depression, the lifetime risk of suicide may be as high as 6%. This compares with a risk of 1.3% in the general population.

⇨ For those with bipolar, suicide risks are high, at 15 times that of the general population.

⇨ Antidepressants can be very effective in helping people to recover from depression, but can also be used to attempt suicide through an overdose. There is no evidence to show that they reduce suicide or self-harm.

⇨ Selective Serotonin Reuptake Inhibitors have been investigated as antidepressant drugs which can cause suicidal thoughts and behaviour in some people. Current research suggests that this is true for children and adolescents but there is no evidence to support the heightened suicide risk in adults.

⇨ Symptoms of depression appear over a period or in the case of manic depression, suddenly and escalate over a few days.

Clinical symptoms and diagnostics

The following are amongst the symptoms cited in cases of major depressive episodes. It is worth noting that these usually develop over days to weeks. In diagnostic terms, five of these should be present during the same two-week period and have caused a change from previous functioning. For a major depressive episode, symptoms must appear on a daily basis and last most of the day or all day.

⇨ Depressed mood (such as feeling sad, empty).

⇨ Markedly diminished pleasure in all (or almost all) activities.

⇨ Insomnia (or hypersomnia).

⇨ Increase/decrease in appetite or significant weight loss.

⇨ Fatigue/loss of energy.

⇨ Feelings of worthlessness.

⇨ Excessive or inappropriate guilt.

⇨ Diminished ability to think, concentrate, and/or take decisions.

⇨ Recurrent thoughts of death, suicidal ideation, having a suicide plan or making a suicide attempt.

Manic episodes typically occur suddenly and symptoms escalate over the course of a few days. In diagnostic terms a person should be experiencing persistently elevated mood for at least one week with three or more of the following symptoms persisting:

⇨ 'Racing' of ideas.

⇨ More talkative than usual.

⇨ Inflated self-esteem.

⇨ Significantly reduced need for sleep.

⇨ Great difficulties concentrating.

⇨ Engagement in activities which appear pleasurable but can lead to painful consequences.

Definitions and types of depression

The term depression covers a wide range of experiences and illnesses, from mild to severe, transient to persistent. Medical classifications and terms are:

⇨ Major depressive disorder – this is more severe and is diagnosed by the person feeling five or more of the symptoms of depression, lasting over two weeks.

⇨ Adjustment disorder – these are milder and shorter-lived forms of depression, often resulting from stressful experiences.

⇨ Dysthymia – covers long-term symptoms of depression (of at least two years) which are not severe enough to meet the criteria for major depression.

⇨ Post-natal depression – which can occur after childbirth (and also peri-natal depression, which

can occur during pregnancy but which is less common).

⇨ Seasonal Affective Disorder (SAD) – which is depression associated with lack of daylight and shorter daylight hours in winter.

⇨ Bipolar disorder (also sometimes called manic depression, or bipolar affective disorder). See below.

⇨ A distinction should be made between the forms of depression which are 'unipolar' including major depression, dysthymia, SAD, and post-natal depression, and 'bipolar' disorder or manic depression. Bipolar depression is a serious mental health problem involving extreme swings of mood (highs and lows). This form of depression occurs in bouts, separated by periods of mania (highs), in which the person may become psychotic and lose touch with reality.

↳ A persistent 'low' mood, with difficult feelings such as guilt, anxiety, sadness;

↳ losing interest or pleasure in things, low self-esteem;

↳ difficulty sleeping or sleeping too much;

↳ tiredness, fatigue;

↳ changes to appetite, and perhaps loss or gain of weight;

↳ difficulty in thinking or concentrating;

↳ recurrent thoughts of death or suicide attempt.

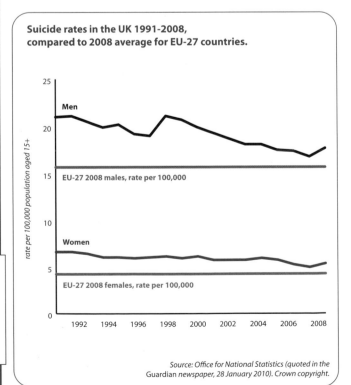

Suicide rates in the UK 1991-2008, compared to 2008 average for EU-27 countries.

Men

EU-27 2008 males, rate per 100,000

Women

EU-27 2008 females, rate per 100,000

rate per 100,000 population aged 15+

Source: Office for National Statistics (quoted in the Guardian newspaper, 28 January 2010). Crown copyright.

⇨ Depression can be due to a shortage of certain chemicals (serotonin, noradrenaline and dopamine) in the brain, which can be triggered in some people by stress.

⇨ The presentation of depression, its meanings and how it is experienced, vary according to culture. The western experience of depression, outlined above, may not hold for people of Asian, Caribbean or other cultures.

Prevalence of unipolar types of depression

⇨ Depression is a very common mental health problem worldwide. The World Health Organization estimates that depression will become the second most common cause of disability worldwide (after heart disease) by 2020.

⇨ In total, about one in six adults are known to have a neurotic mental health disorder in any given week. The most common disorder is mixed anxiety and depression (8.8%).

⇨ Major depression affects one in 20 people during their lifetime. Both major depression and dysthymia appear to be more common in women.

⇨ In Britain, 3–4% of men and 7–8% of women suffer from moderate to severe depression at any one time.

⇨ Women are twice as likely to be diagnosed and treated for depression. However, it is believed that men suffer depression to a larger extent than the statistics show, since men are less likely to seek medical help and when they do, doctors are less likely to detect depressive symptoms.

⇨ In North America, increased use or abuse of alcohol and other drugs amongst men is now being viewed as a 'masked' symptom of depression.

⇨ Only 20% of people suffering from depression actually go to their doctor with an emotional problem. The vast majority complain of nonspecific symptoms such as headache, tiredness or vague abdominal pains. This type of 'masked' depression is more common in older people, who may feel embarrassed about their condition.

⇨ An international study in ten countries found that rates of major depression in the community varied from 1.5% in Taiwan to 19% in Beirut. The average age when people began to experience depression was between 25 and 35 years. In every country, rates of major depression among women were higher than those among men.

⇨ Depression is the most common psychiatric disorder in later life. 10–15% of the population aged 65 years or over suffer from significant depressive symptoms.

SAMARITANS

⇨ Depression is relatively rare in children. Prevalence figures for major depression are 0.3% in pre-school children, 1.8% before puberty, and 5–9% in adolescents. The female:male gender ratio is equal prior to puberty but among adolescents depression is more common in females.

⇨ Dysthymia tends to develop early in a person's life during childhood to early adulthood, but most people delay approximately ten years before seeking treatment. Like all forms of unipolar depression, dysthymia affects more women than men. At any point in time, 3–5% of the population may be affected with dysthymia, within a lifetime approximately 6% are affected.

⇨ In western Europe the prevalence for post-natal depression is 13%.

Prevalence of bipolar depression

⇨ Bipolar depression is rarer than unipolar forms, affects men and women equally and affects about five people in 1,000, or 0.5% of the population in the UK. It often first occurs when work, study, family or emotional pressures are at their greatest. In women it can also be triggered by childbirth or during the menopause.

In western Europe the prevalence for post-natal depression is 13%

⇨ Age at onset of bipolar disorder is earlier than that for major depression. Research suggests it starts six years earlier.

Suicide risk

⇨ For people diagnosed with major depression, the lifetime risk of suicide may be as high as 6%, although this figure may be more applicable to those who have been admitted to hospital as a result of depression. For people seen as outpatients or treated by GPs, risks are much lower.

⇨ For those with bipolar disorder the suicide risk is much higher, at 15 times that of the general population. This risk is further increased by a previous suicide attempt and by alcohol abuse.

⇨ Every week 10% of the UK population aged 16–65 report significant depressive symptoms, and one in ten of these admits to suicidal thinking.

↳ Previous self-harm.

↳ Severity of the illness.

↳ Alcohol or drugs abuse.

↳ Serious or chronic physical illnesses.

↳ Schizophrenia.

⇨ Research shows that depression is one of the most frequent mental health problems in people who die by suicide. This is also true of young people; major depression is common amongst adolescents who have overdosed.

⇨ Other factors may be important, either independently or in combination with depression, in the development of suicidal thoughts and behaviour in an individual. Such factors include impulsiveness, aggressiveness, addiction, suicide or suicide attempts in close relatives, divorce, separation and parental discord.

⇨ Depression is common amongst people who self-harm, both in those who habitually self-harm by, for example, self-cutting, without suicidal intent and in those who may have suicidal intent when they self-harm.

⇨ In people who have self-harmed, depression and impulsivity have been shown to be strongly associated with the strength of the intent to die by suicide.

⇨ Major, or severe, depression in adolescence is associated with higher risk of both suicide attempting and death by suicide in adulthood.

⇨ Although dysthymia in itself is not related to suicide, 10% of those suffering from it will go on to develop major depression.

⇨ Severe post-natal depression is linked to elevated suicide risk, despite the fact that in general, women who have recently given birth are at low risk of suicide. Those who are admitted to hospital for very severe post-natal depression can be up to 70 times as likely to die by suicide. Risks are especially high in the first year after childbirth.

Major, or severe, depression in adolescence is associated with higher risk of both suicide attempting and death by suicide in adulthood

⇨ Depression is generally recognised as a feature of suicide in schizophrenia, where the greatest risk of suicide comes during non-psychotic, depressed phases of the illness. In a survey of 390 schizophrenia patients over a 13-year period, 19 (5%) took their own lives. However, research suggests that the seriousness of suicidal intent is related to hopelessness about the future, which is one particular aspect of depression.

Antidepressants and suicide

Antidepressants are the main mode of treatment for depression by general practitioners, and their usage continues to increase. Annually in the UK, GPs spend £160m per year on antidepressant drugs. In 2002 33 million prescriptions were dispensed in the UK (16 million in 1995).

⇨ Whereas many depressed people are helped to recovery by medication, and the rise in prescribing of antidepressants coincides with a fall in national suicide rates, there is as yet no convincing evidence that antidepressants prevent suicide.

⇨ It is also common for people to kill themselves by overdosing on antidepressants. 15% of overdoses involve antidepressant medication and there were substantial increases in self-poisoning with antidepressants between 1985 and 1997 in the UK.

⇨ Using antidepressants to overdose is more common in people who repeatedly self-harm or attempt suicide, and in older people.

⇨ Since depression is such a common factor in suicide, a study on the small Swedish island of Gotland attempted to measure the effects on suicide rates of intensively educating GPs to recognise and treat suicide with antidepressants. Results suggested that the programme resulted in a decrease in suicides in depressed women but no change in suicide rates in depressed men. However, further research in England failed to replicate these effects.

Selective Serotonin Reuptake Inhibitors and Suicide

Newer antidepressants, called Selective Serotonin Reuptake Inhibitors (SSRIs), have lower mortality in overdose (whether purposeful or accidental) than older drugs. Older antidepressants include tricyclics and monoamine oxidase inhibitors (MAOIs).

⇨ There has been some controversy over the relation between SSRIs and suicidal thoughts and behaviour, particularly in young people and children, which has led to guidelines advising against prescription of SSRIs to those under the age of 18 in the UK.

⇨ One study has provided some evidence to suggest that SSRIs are associated with an increased risk of suicidal behaviour in children and that most SSRIs seem to be ineffective for childhood depression. However, the authors point out that further, longer-term studies are required to assess the overall effect on population health of the recent rise in antidepressant use.

⇨ Another study failed to show any difference between different types of antidepressant medication and subsequent suicides. It did show, however, that suicide risk was highest in the early days of beginning to take any antidepressant. The authors felt that this was likely to be because people seeking help do so at the worst stages of their depression, and antidepressants are not immediately effective, so there is a higher risk in people who have been newly diagnosed and treated, compared with those who have been treated for some time.

Other treatments

⇨ In bipolar disorder, Lithium has been shown to be an effective treatment which lowers the risk of suicide.

⇨ Problem-solving therapy has been shown to help people who self-harm with depression, hopelessness and problems. As yet it has not been shown to reduce repeated self-harm.

⇨ The above information is taken from the Samaritans information sheet *Depression and Suicide* and is reprinted with permission. Visit www.samaritans.org for more information or to view references for this piece.

© *Samaritans*

SAMARITANS

Teenage depression

Information from Boots WebMD.

Do you ever wonder whether your irritable or unhappy adolescent might actually be experiencing teenage depression? Of course, most teenagers feel unhappy at times. When you add hormone havoc to the many other changes happening in a teenager's life, it's easy to see why their moods swing like a pendulum. Yet studies have shown that two per cent of teenagers in the UK suffer from depression. Depression and the serious problems associated with it can be treated. So if your teenager's unhappiness lasts for more than two weeks and they display other symptoms of depression, it may be time to seek help from a health professional.

Why do adolescents get depression?

There are many reasons why a teenager might become depressed. For example, teenagers can develop feelings of worthlessness and inadequacy over their school marks. School performance, social status with peers, sexual orientation or family life can each have a major effect on how a teenager feels. Sometimes, teenage depression may result from environmental stress. Whatever the cause, when friends or family, or things that the teenager usually enjoys, don't help to improve their sadness or sense of isolation, there's a good chance that they have teenage depression.

What are the symptoms of teenage depression?

Often, teenagers suffering from depression will have a noticeable change in their thinking and behaviour. They may have no motivation and even become withdrawn, closing their bedroom door after school and staying in their room for hours.

Teenagers suffering from depression may sleep excessively, change their eating habits, and may even exhibit criminal behaviour such as vandalism or shoplifting. Here are more signs of depression in adolescents, even though they may or may not show all signs:

⇨ Apathy.

⇨ Complaints of pain, including headaches, stomach aches, lower back pain or fatigue.

⇨ Difficulty concentrating.

⇨ Difficulty making decisions.

⇨ Excessive or inappropriate guilt.

⇨ Irresponsible behaviour; for example, forgetting obligations, being late for classes, bunking off school.

⇨ Loss of interest in food or compulsive overeating that results in rapid weight loss or gain.

⇨ Memory loss.

⇨ Preoccupation with death and dying.

⇨ Rebellious behaviour.

⇨ Sadness, anxiety, or a feeling of hopelessness.

⇨ Staying awake at night and sleeping during the day.

⇨ Sudden drop in marks at school.

⇨ Use of alcohol or drugs and promiscuous sexual activity.

⇨ Withdrawal from friends.

Can teenage depression run in families?

Yes. Depression, which usually starts between the ages of 15 and 30, runs in families. In fact, teenage depression may be more common among adolescents who have a family history of depression.

How is teenage depression diagnosed?

There aren't any specific medical tests that can detect depression. Healthcare professionals determine if a teenager is suffering from depression by conducting interviews and psychological tests with the teenager and their family members, teachers and peers.

The severity of the teenage depression and the risk of suicide are determined based on the assessment of these interviews. Treatment recommendations are also made based on the data collected from the interviews.

The doctor will also look for signs of potentially co-existing psychiatric disorders such as anxiety, mania or schizophrenia. The doctor will also assess the teenager for risks of suicidal or homicidal behaviours. Incidence of attempted suicide and self-mutilation is higher in females than males while completed suicide is higher in males. One of the most vulnerable groups for completed suicide is the 18–24 age group.

BOOTS WEBMD

How is teenage depression treated?

There are a variety of methods used to treat depression, including medications and psychotherapy. Family counselling may be helpful if family conflict is contributing to a teenager's depression. The teenager will also need support from family or teachers to help with any school or peer problems. Occasionally, hospitalisation in a psychiatric unit may be required for teenagers with severe depression.

Your mental health care provider will determine the best course of treatment for your teenager.

Does depression medicine work for teenage depression?

Yes. A large number of research trials have shown the effectiveness of depression medications in relieving the symptoms of teenage depression. One key recent study, funded by the National Institute of Mental Health, reviewed three different approaches to treating adolescents with moderate to severe depression:

⇨ One approach was using the antidepressant medication fluoxetine, which is approved by the FDA for use with paediatric patients ages eight to 18.

⇨ The second treatment was using cognitive behavioural therapy, or CBT, to help the teenager recognise and change negative patterns of thinking that may increase symptoms of depression.

⇨ The third approach was a combination of medication and CBT.

At the end of the 12-week study, researchers found that nearly three out of every four patients who received the combination treatment, depression medication and psychotherapy significantly improved. More than 60% of those who took antidepressants alone improved.

The study confirmed that combination treatment was nearly twice as effective in relieving depression as psychotherapy alone.

What are the warning signs for teenager suicide?

Teenage suicide is a serious problem.

Family difficulties, the loss of a loved one or perceived failures at school or in relationships can all lead to negative feelings and depression. Teenage depression often makes problems seem overwhelming and the associated pain unbearable. Suicide is an act of desperation and teenage depression is often the root cause.

Warning signs of suicide with teenage depression include:

⇨ Expressing hopelessness for the future.

⇨ Giving up on one's self, talking as if no one else cares.

⇨ Preparing for death, giving away favourite possessions, writing goodbye letters, or making a will.

⇨ Starting to use/abuse drugs or alcohol to aid sleep or for relief from their mental anguish.

⇨ Threatening to kill one's self.

If your teenager displays any of these behaviours, you should seek help from a mental healthcare professional immediately. Or you can call a suicide hotline for help.

Depression carries a high risk of suicide. Anybody who expresses suicidal thoughts or intentions should be taken very, very seriously. Do not hesitate to call a suicide hotline immediately. Call Samaritans UK: 08457 90 90 90; ROI: 1850 60 90 90; and/or ChildLine 0800 11 11.

What can parents do to alleviate teenage depression?

Parenting teenagers can be very challenging. There are, though, some effective parenting and communication techniques you can use to help lower the stress level for your teenager:

⇨ When disciplining your teenager, replace shame and punishment with positive reinforcement for good behaviour. Shame and punishment can make an adolescent feel worthless and inadequate.

⇨ Allow your teenager to make mistakes. Overprotecting or making decisions for teenagers can be perceived as a lack of faith in their abilities. This can make them feel less confident.

⇨ Give your teenager breathing room. Don't expect teenagers to do exactly as you say all of the time.

⇨ Do not force your teenager down a path you wanted to follow. Avoid trying to relive your youth through your teenager's activities and experiences.

⇨ If you suspect that your teenager is depressed, take

the time to listen to their concerns. Even if you don't think the problem is of real concern, remember that it may feel very real to someone who is growing up.

⇨ Keep the lines of communication open, even if your teenager seems to want to withdraw.

⇨ Try to avoid telling your teenager what to do. Instead, listen closely and you may discover more about the issues causing the problems.

If you feel overwhelmed or unable to reach your teenager, or if you continue to be concerned, seek help from a qualified healthcare professional.

Can't teenage depression go away without medical treatment?

Teenage depression tends to come and go in episodes. Once a teenager has one bout of depression, they are likely to get depressed again at some point. The consequence of letting teenage depression go untreated can be extremely serious, even deadly.

WebMD Medical Reference

Sources

⇨ National Institute of Mental Health: 'What is Depression?'

⇨ Food and Drug Administration: 'The Lowdown on Depression'.

⇨ Mental Health America: 'Factsheet: Depression in Teens'.

⇨ Medline Plus: 'Adolescent Depression'.

⇨ ParentsMedGuide.org: 'The Use of Medication in Treating Childhood and Adolescent Depression: Information for Patients and Families'.

⇨ SAMHSA: 'Major Depression in Children and Adolescents'.

⇨ Medline Plus: 'Teen Mental Health'.

⇨ American Psychiatric Association, Practice Guideline for the Treatment of Patients with Major Depression, 2000.

⇨ American Psychiatric Association. Diagnostic and Statistical Manual of Mental Disorders: DSM-IV-TR, American Psychiatric Pub, 2000.

⇨ Dr Fieve, R, Bipolar II, Rodale Books, 2006.

⇨ Mind: 'Suicide Rates, Risks and Prevention Strategies'.

⇨ NHS Choices: 'Depression Overview'.

Reviewed by Dr Rob Hicks on 1 June 2009

⇨ Reproduced with permission from Boots WebMD. Visit www.webmd.boots.com for more information.

Statistics about young adults with mental health problems

According to the 2001 Census, there are 7,159,694 16- to 25-year-olds in the UK. This amounts to 12% of the UK's population. 2,909,760 or about 5% of the total UK population are between 16 and 19 years old and 4,249,934 or about 7% of the total UK population are aged between 20 and 25 years old.

Mental health problems

⇨ 1.7% of 16- to 19-year-olds and 2.2% of 20- to 24-year-olds, or about 127,000, have suffered from a depressive episode.

⇨ 13.3% of 16- to 19-year-olds and 15.8% 20- to 24-year-olds in Great Britain are reported to suffer from a neurotic disorder.

⇨ About 0.2% of 16- to 24-year-olds have a probable psychotic disorder.

⇨ 0.9% of 16- to 19-year-olds and 1.9% of 20- to 24-year-olds suffer from Obsessive Compulsive Disorder.

⇨ 3.4% of 16- to 34-year-olds have been diagnosed with a personality disorder.

⇨ The suicide rate in the UK among 15- to 24-year-olds in 2004 was 11.9 per 100,000 in young men, and 3.6 per 100,000 in young women.

⇨ Overall, the suicide rate has fallen from the peak in 1998 of 18.1 per 100,000 in young men and 4.5 per 100,000 in young women.

⇨ In England and Wales during 2003, accidents of any kind were the main cause of death in young men aged between 15 and 34, and suicide and injury/poisoning of undetermined intent was the second.

⇨ In 2003, 1,075 young men aged 15 to 34, and 273 young women of the same age range, died as a result of committing suicide/poisoning of undetermined intent.

⇨ Suicide and injury/poisoning of undetermined intent was the third highest cause of death in young women aged 15 to 34 years.

⇨ In 1998–2004 the suicide rate for young men aged 15 to 34 in England was 19.1 per 100,000 population. The suicide rate of young men of the same age group in Scotland was 36.9, which is almost double that of England.

⇨ Information from YoungMinds. Visit www.youngminds.org.uk for more information.

© *YoungMinds*

BOOTS WEBMD / YOUNGMINDS

Living with depression

Depression, self-harm and suicidal feelings.

Self-harm is purposeful injury or harm to oneself. For some people self-harm is a way of dealing with very difficult thoughts and feelings that they can't cope with in more positive ways. Many young people self-harm and it is thought that about one in ten people in the UK have self-harmed. Not everyone with depression self-harms, and similarly, many young people who self-harm are not depressed. Self-harm can also be a suicidal act, although not everyone who self-harms is suicidal. Those who self-harm may be at a higher risk from suicide though.

Here, young people talk about self-harming, how it started, their motives for self-harm and the support they had received from family, peers and professionals. Some young people we spoke with had also experienced suicidal feelings or had attempted suicide and here, they talk about those experiences and how to get help if feeling suicidal.

Beginning

A few people remembered starting to first self-harm at the age of nine and ten but most started self-harming in their teens. Those who had started at a younger age said they didn't necessarily realise at the time that it was 'self-harm' but more just about causing physical pain, or as one woman described, 'being accident-prone'.

Quite a few people also said that self-harm had started off with what they described as harmless 'scratches' but had gradually become worse and more frequent, leading to injuries and for a few, permanent physical bodily damage. These people said they had never intended self-harm to become a regular thing but that they had become 'obsessed' or 'addicted' to it over time. One woman said it was 'never meant to go that far' and another that it had just 'spun out of control'.

Making sense of self-harm

Young people described how complex self-harming was and talked about the wide-ranging reasons behind their behaviour. Many said they were very aware of the reasons why they were self-harming at the time of doing it, rather than it being a random act.

Many people described self-harm as 'a form of control'. For them, it was a way to control or contain what otherwise felt like uncontrollable feelings of upset and depression, or an 'overwhelming' life. In this sense, self-harming was like 'a bad coping strategy' for young people who didn't know how else to ease their pain.

Similarly, many also described it as 'a release' of pain, upset, stress or anger. One woman said for her, self-harm was the only way to 'express her feelings' and another one described it as a way to 'let out the pain inside'. A couple of people compared the effects of self-harming to crying; a release of tension and sadness. When they were unable to shed tears they would self-harm. For many, self-harming was closely connected to depression and they said they self-harmed because they felt so low and down. Some said they only self-harmed during depressive episodes and bad periods of life. In turn, scars from self-harm could then make depression worse and make people feel bad or ashamed about themselves and their bodies. Many young people also said that self-harming was like an addiction, and compared it to smoking or drugs.

Many people described self-harm as 'a form of control'

For some people, self-harming was about punishing themselves and causing pain and injury because they felt so low and negative about themselves. A couple of people said they felt unable to deal with 'extreme emotions', especially happiness, and hence self-harmed as a way to 'balance out' their emotions.

People also pointed out that sometimes, and in some ways, self-harming was a way to seek attention. They wanted to clearly distinguish between seeking attention for the sake of it, and seeking attention as a way to get help. One man described his self-harming as 'cries for help'. A couple of people emphasised that 'attention seeking' through self-destructive behaviour is always a problem and may be the only way for someone to seek help.

Other people's reactions

People felt there was a general lack of understanding about self-harm. Many felt criticised and judged for doing it. They had experienced people staring at the scars, whispering behind their backs or openly making fun of them. Many wanted to keep the scars or marks hidden at first but said in time they had learnt to accept them as a part of themselves and their past and didn't want to hide them anymore. Some had been approached by strangers on the street or in the pub commenting on or questioning their behaviour.

Those whose parents had found out about self-harming said their parents didn't quite know how to handle the situation. Many said their parents had been really worried for them and also upset when they found out. Some parents had blamed themselves for young people's

self-harming, others had got angry. Many parents had also been very helpful and supportive, trying to speak with young people or help them to go for counselling. A couple of women said their partners or parents had been so desperate for them to stop that they'd tried to physically restrain them.

Some people felt that professionals and even hospital staff were unsure how to handle self-harming or how to best help young people. A couple said their schools had been aware of the self-harm. One person said the school completely ignored the problem whereas another one had great support from college, including flexibility around assignments and deadlines when needed.

A few people also expressed worries about their work prospects and how visible scars might affect their future employment. A couple of them worked with children or wanted to do a course in childcare. One woman felt it might be inappropriate for her to work with children who would see the scars and another said in her work she always covers the scars.

Many wanted to keep self-harming a secret and hide it from family members, for example

People described self-harming as something directed internally towards themselves and wanted to dispel the myth that people who self-harm would be a danger or a risk to other people.

Getting support for self-harming

There is a lot of support available for self-harm and many people we spoke with said they'd been keen to stop. All the people said they were very aware that self-harming was 'bad' for them but it wasn't so simple to just stop. One woman compared self-harming to smoking and said:

'Like smoking it's an addiction and just saying, "Right I want it to stop now, and that's it." It doesn't really work like that I'm afraid.'

Many wanted to keep self-harming a secret and hide it from family members, for example. A few said they themselves hadn't seen self-harm as a problem straight away but only much later. Several people had looked for help, but said that stopping self-harming had been difficult and often a long process. One woman said that after years of resorting to self-harm it was very hard to learn to 'cope without it'.

There were tips the people had been given to help them to try and control the urge to self-harm. These included squeezing an ice cube in their hand or flicking themselves with rubber bands. Some people found that distracting themselves by, for example, listening to music, reading or going out helped them occupy their mind so that they weren't consumed by thoughts of self-harm.

Commonly, people felt there was very little information, support and knowledge about self-harm. Some had been to counselling for depression and had been able to process the issue of self-harm too but said they were given no information specific to self-harm. A few had also looked out for information actively themselves, read self-help books and a couple of people had found good support websites and forums for people who self-harm. However, one woman also pointed out that going on the websites sometimes got her down and made the urge to self-harm worse rather than better.

Suicidal feelings

A few young people we spoke with had experienced suicidal feelings or had attempted suicide. Some described having suicidal 'thoughts' or 'urges' but said they would never act on them. For them, it was more an aspect of their negative or pessimistic mindset. Some described suicide attempts more as a way to harm or hurt themselves than to end their lives, and a couple of people compared a suicide attempt to self-harm in the sense of attempting to exercise control over their life.

A couple of the people who had attempted suicide made a distinction between those attempts which were serious 'cries for help' and the ones when they had really wanted to end their lives. Those who had attempted suicide several times said it had become a cycle, and they often ended up back in A&E.

People who had suicidal thoughts described having felt 'utterly hopeless', like they lacked a future or the desire to live. A couple had had a 'breakdown' or felt that they'd struggled a long time and had 'had enough'. Some said they felt like a 'burden' or 'baggage' to others. For most, a suicide attempt had been an accumulation of several things going wrong at school, at home and in relationships. For some, it had involved problems with alcohol and drugs and long-term depression.

The process of getting over suicidal behaviour had been long and gradual but successful for many. Most had been admitted to hospital, for emergency crisis care as a minimum, or for a longer stay on the ward. People pointed out that it was the underlying urges of suicidal thoughts which needed to be tackled, rather than just the acts themselves. This way they had felt able to regain control over their lives and to rebuild their lives. Taking the first step to get the help and speak about what they were feeling had been the hardest but the best step young people said they had taken.

⇨ Information from youthhealthtalk.org. Visit www. youthhealthtalk.org for more information.

© *youthhealthtalk.org*

Teenage depression no longer on the increase

The overall level of teenage mental health problems is no longer on the increase and may even be in decline, according to new research published by the Nuffield Foundation.

There was no rise in the level of emotional problems such as anxiety and depression amongst 11- to 15-year-olds between 1999 and 2004. In the same period there was a slight decrease in the level of conduct problems such as lying and disobedience. This follows a 25-year period in which the rate of all these problems had risen dramatically (from 1974 to 1999).

The research was undertaken by Dr Stephan Collishaw from Cardiff University and Professor Barbara Maughan from the Institute of Psychiatry. The researchers analysed data on the mental health of 11- to 15-year-olds using Office of National Statistics surveys from 1999 and 2004. The research updates an earlier Nuffield Foundation study, *Time Trends in Adolescent Mental Health* (2004), which identified a significant increase in teenage mental health problems and led to a Government commitment to fundamentally reform children's mental health services.

The researchers looked at the level of emotional and conduct problems as identified by parents. The main findings are:

⇨ There was no change in the amount of emotional problems such as anxiety or depression between 1999 and 2004 (these problems rose by 70% in the preceding 25 years from 1974 to 1999).

⇨ Parent reports of conduct problems such as lying, stealing, disobedience and fighting decreased slightly between 1999 and 2004 (these problems doubled between 1974 and 1999).

⇨ Researchers looked at nine different measures of mental health problems in 1999 and 2004, as identified by parents, teachers and teenagers. Of these nine measures, eight had decreased or stayed the same. The exception was the level of emotional problems reported by teachers, which increased slightly.

⇨ Although teenage mental health problems did not increase between 1999 and 2004, the dramatic rise in these problems prior to 1999 means that today's teenagers are still more likely to experience emotional and conduct problems than teenagers in the 1970s and 1980s.

Dr Collishaw said:

'The level of mental health problems amongst UK teenagers, which increased at an alarming rate over the 25 years from 1974 to 1999, has now reached a plateau. What is not yet clear is whether the slight decrease in levels of some problems is the start of a trend in the opposite direction.'

The research findings are published in a Nuffield Foundation briefing paper, *Time Trends in Adolescent Well-being*. The study is part of a series designed to examine the changes in adolescent mental health over time and the reasons for those changes. Research published earlier this year ruled out a link between the mental health of teenagers and a decline in parenting, as evidence suggests parenting may have improved since the 1970s. Other research currently underway includes changes in the way teenagers spend their time; drug and alcohol use; neighbourhood and community; stress, and school transitions.

18 December 2009

⇨ The above information is a press release from the Nuffield Foundation based on the findings of research it commissioned. Visit www.nuffieldfoundation.org for more information.

© Nuffield Foundation

When a seven-minute diagnosis is not enough

By Clare Allan

GPs have difficulty recognising depression in their patients, according to an overview of more than 40 studies conducted by the University of Leicester. The research, involving more than 50,000 patients, found that GPs correctly picked up on depression in only 50% of cases. They were actually more likely to misdiagnose a patient as depressed than they were to spot a case of genuine depression.

Statistics concerning mental health must always be treated with caution. Depression does not show up on an x-ray after all; a diagnosis cannot be confirmed or excluded by means of a blood test. Psychiatrists regularly disagree concerning the diagnoses of patients and a growing number are starting to question the helpfulness of such labels at all when it comes to trying to understand and treat an individual's problems. One wonders what 'gold standard' was used to measure the success of the hapless GPs.

That said, there are undoubtedly challenges facing both GPs and their patients when it comes to dealing with issues of mental health. The relationship is a crucial one, not least because it's GPs who prescribe the medication. They do lots of other things too, of course, such as providing access to specialist help, but even once someone has been referred to the community mental health team, or is seeing a psychiatrist regularly, it is still the GP who prescribes the medication.

The reasons for this are obvious. It's important to have a single doctor, a 'general' practitioner, with an overview of the whole of a patient's care. The fact that someone has mental health problems does not, unfortunately, exempt them from physical illness. Medications can interact. An unfortunate consequence of the system, however, is that unless a good enough relationship exists between a mental health patient and their GP, they may, especially at times of crisis, stop taking their medication. If a visit to the doctor feels unmanageable, they may try to spin out what meds they have left by reducing the dose, stop altogether, or self-prescribe via the Internet. I know, I've tried all three.

Given that none of these options seems especially advisable, it's worth considering what makes the difference between a positive visit and an unrepeatable one. The mental health charity Rethink, in collaboration with the Royal College of General Practitioners, has produced a toolkit for GPs, which can be downloaded from the charity's website. The report, *What's reasonable?*, highlights the problems that service users commonly face in accessing GPs and suggests adjustments that might be made to help them. In the same way that a wheelchair ramp may be needed for physically disabled patients, practices need to think about how their booking systems, appointments, waiting areas and practice staff may impact with those with serious mental illness.

> ### GPs correctly picked up on depression in only 50% of cases

But the clincher is what happens when you see the GP. Despite the fact that an estimated one-third of GP appointments are mental health-related, the system is much better suited to physical illness. While a nippy GP may just about be able to take a temperature, peer down a throat and type out a prescription in the seven-minute average consultation time, diagnosing mental health problems is likely to take much longer. What's really needed is an ongoing relationship, an opportunity for both doctor and patient to develop a sense of each other.

Unfortunately, things seem to be going in the opposite direction. The increasing use of same-day appointment systems makes it extremely difficult to see the same GP consistently, at least in a large group practice. At my last surgery I saw five different doctors in less than a year; my sole objective quickly became to get my prescription and get the hell out.

My experience at my new practice is quite different. So far I've seen the same GP on three successive occasions. I've spoken to her on the phone and she's talked to my psychiatrist. That's never happened before. My only real concern is that her name is not on the list of doctors in reception. It worries me each time I go, but I'm keeping my fingers crossed.

⇨ The GP toolkit is at rethink/GPtoolkit.

⇨ Clare Allan is an author and writes on mental health issues.

5 August 2009

THE GUARDIAN

Antidepressants

TheSite.org identifies the different antidepressant drugs available and explores their pros and cons.

How do antidepressants work?

Depression is associated with low levels of certain chemicals in the brain, notably serotonin and noradrenaline. Most antidepressant drugs are designed to increase the levels of these chemicals in the brain. Antidepressants are not a quick-fix solution as they can take between two to four weeks before they start to work. A minimum course of six months' treatment is usually recommended in order to ensure that a relapse does not occur. Antidepressants can be very effective at lifting people's mood and alleviate the distressing symptoms of depression; however, they do not address any underlying emotional or psychological cause of why a person became depressed in the first place. Due to this, many people are referred for talking treatments as well as being prescribed drug treatment.

Depression is associated with low levels of certain chemicals in the brain

Who takes them?

Antidepressant drugs are used primarily in the treatment of depression, but are also used to treat other conditions such as anxiety, panic attacks, obsessive-compulsive disorder and phobias.

Are there any possible side effects?

Drugs can affect people differently; what works well for one person may not for another. Some people may experience adverse effects from a medication while others have little or no problem. Common side effects of antidepressant drugs can include dry mouth, blurred vision, nausea, sweating, constipation or diarrhoea, sexual problems, rashes, anxiety, tremor, dizziness, or drowsiness. Less common side effects include hallucinations, suicidal thoughts, mania, convulsions and movement disorders. A frequent side effect of Prozac is that it can interfere with your ability to orgasm. Of course if you aren't in a relationship, you may not mind, but if you are, sex may be an important way for you to get pleasure, so you may decide to ask to switch to another brand. If you experience worrying side effects, it is important to discuss these concerns with your doctor (GP), who could try prescribing you a different drug that may not have adverse effects for you. Alcohol and recreational drugs should be avoided as they can interact with the medication or cause it to be less effective.

Can they cause dependence?

Although it is generally claimed that antidepressants do not cause dependence, it is usually recommended that the drugs be withdrawn gradually. Stopping taking drugs suddenly can cause a 'discontinuation syndrome' with physical symptoms such as nausea, vomiting, diarrhoea, flu-like symptoms or sleep problems. People can also experience 'rebound depression', a recurrence of the depressed feelings as a result of not withdrawing from antidepressants slowly.

What are the choices?

There are many different drugs that can be prescribed depending on an individual's particular situation, their diagnosis, and the severity of their symptoms. Some can have sedative effects, others can stimulate; some are prescribed widely, others usually only within a hospital environment. Your doctor will probably recommend which drug they think is likely to work well for you, but remember you have the right to make an informed decision about which treatment to have and whether or not to accept the treatment a doctor suggests. Below is a list of commonly available antidepressants and the conditions they are usually recommended to treat. Remember, drugs tend to have two names, a generic name for the drug itself, and a brand name given by a particular manufacturer.

SSRIs (Serotonin Specific Re-uptake Inhibitors)

⇨ Citalopram (Cipramil): depression, panic disorder

⇨ Escitalopram (Cipralex): depression, panic disorder

⇨ Fluoxetine (Prozac): depression, obsessive-compulsive disorder

⇨ Fluvoxamine (Faverin): depression, obsessive-compulsive disorder

⇨ Paroxetine (Seroxat): depression, anxiety, panic, social phobia

⇨ Sertraline (Lustral): depression, obsessive-compulsive disorder

SNRI (Serotonin-Noradrenaline Re-uptake Inhibitor)

⇨ Venlafaxine (Efexor): depression, anxiety

NARI (Noradrenaline Re-uptake Inhibitor)

⇨ Reboxetine (Edronax): depression

NaSSA (Noradenergic and Specific Serotonergic Antidepressant)

⇨ Mirtazepine (Zispin): depression

MAOIs (Monoamine Oxidase Inhibitors)

⇨ Phenelzine (Nardil): depression

⇨ Isocarboxazid (Isocarboxazid non-proprietary): depression

⇨ Tranylcypromine (Tranylcypromine non-proprietary): depression

Reversible MAOI

⇨ Moclobemide (Manerix): depression, social phobia

Tricyclic antidepressants

⇨ Maprotiline (Ludiomil): depression

⇨ Mianserin Hydrochloride (Mianserin): depression

⇨ Trazodone (Molipaxin): depression, anxiety

Other antidepressant drugs

⇨ Flupenthixol (Fluanxol): depression, psychosis

⇨ Tryptophan (Optimax): hospital treatment of severe depression

Herbal supplements

⇨ St John's Wort (Hypericum perforatum): depression

Who shouldn't take antidepressants?

If you fall into one of the following categories, consultation with your doctor is especially important, and you may be advised to avoid medication altogether:

⇨ Pregnant women: the mother's needs will always be taken into consideration, but every alternative should be explored before prescribing antidepressants.

⇨ Breastfeeding mums: there is a possible risk to an unborn child, and breastfeeding mums can pass any drugs they are taking to their babies through their breast milk.

⇨ Children: guidelines on depression in children and young people recommend that antidepressants should only be given to children in combination with psychological therapies.

⇨ Those on other medication: antidepressants can interact with a number of different types of drug, and some combinations can be dangerous, so make sure your doctor is aware of any other drugs you are taking.

⇨ Heavy drinkers: taking antidepressants could be detrimental as alcohol is a depressant and the two interact badly.

⇨ The above information is reprinted with kind permission from TheSite. Visit www.thesite.org for more.

© TheSite

Depression sufferers 'not seeking help'

Information from Turning Point.

Nearly three-quarters of people in the UK experience depression occasionally, according to a recent survey from Turning Point.

The mental health charity found that of these, only a third will actually seek help.

Tim Watkins, director of Journeys, which offers support to people affected by depression, said there were two major reasons why people do not seek help for depression.

'The main one is that there is still a gap in public awareness of the symptoms and warning signs of depression. People tend to realise that there is something amiss, they're not feeling that great but they tend not to relate it to depression.

'The second thing is that there's a lot of fear around mental health and mental illness which causes people to avoid seeking help anyway.'

He added that money worries including debt and unemployment were the main causes of depression at the moment.

Mr Watkin's comments echo a recent survey from Aviva which found that 'recession depression' was becoming an increasingly common problem in the workplace as people worried and stressed about employment issues.

2 February 2010

⇨ The above information is reprinted with kind permission from Turning Point. Visit www.turning-point.co.uk for more information.

© Turning Point

THESITE.ORG / TURNING POINT

Talking treatment

Psychological therapies can help to explore what may have contributed to your depression in the first place.

Although medication can help lift your mood, it does not tackle any underlying problems you may be experiencing. Psychological therapies can help to explore what may have contributed to your depression in the first place, and what might be keeping you depressed.

There are lots of different psychological therapies. None have been proven to be 'better' than any other, and so it is more a question of finding a therapy, and therapist, which suits you. Your GP may be able to advise you, and also let you know which therapies are available in your area. All sorts of therapies are available on the NHS, but be prepared for waiting lists. If you decide to choose private therapy, make sure that you select a registered or accredited therapist.

The most common kinds of psychological therapies are:

Cognitive Therapy

How you think largely determines how you feel; when you are depressed, you feel very negative. Cognitive Therapy works by challenging these negative thought patterns, and suggesting changes to destructive behaviour.

Interpersonal therapy

This focuses on your relationships with other people. It teaches you how to communicate more effectively and improve your view of yourself.

Psychodynamic Therapy

This helps people to understand past conflicts, release aggression and reduce feelings of guilt or inadequacy.

Counselling

The term refers to a wide range of techniques and approaches, some of which draw from the above therapies. As a general rule, counselling offers people the opportunity to talk through issues in their everyday lives that may be contributing towards their depression, rather than aiming to treat more deep-rooted problems.

⇨ The above information is reprinted with kind permission from Depression Alliance Scotland. Visit their website at www.dascot.org for more information.

© Depression Alliance Scotland

NHS should use meditation to treat depression, says report

Information from Nursing Times.

The NHS should offer meditation to treat long-term depression, a mental health charity has said.

The Mental Health Foundation published a report stating that annual savings of £7.5bn could be made to the cost of treating depression if the therapy was rolled-out across GPs' surgeries.

Mindfulness-based cognitive therapy (MBCT) is already recommended for recurrent depression by NICE, which reviews the cost effectiveness of NHS treatments.

NICE made the recommendation in 2004 after studies suggested that MBCT could halve depression relapse rates.

However, despite the backing, only a fifth of GPs say they can access the treatment for their patients at present, according to the charity's report *Be Mindful*.

Under MBCT, patients get an eight-week course of two-hour sessions combining meditation with orthodox 'thought training' at an average cost of £300.

Dr Andrew McCulloch, chief executive of the Mental Health Foundation, said: 'Mindfulness-based therapy could be helping to prevent thousands of people from relapsing into depression every year. This would have huge knock-on benefits both socially and economically, making it a sensible treatment to be making available, even at a time when money is short within the NHS.'

5 January 2010

⇨ The above information is reprinted with kind permission from *Nursing Times*. Visit www.nursingtimes.net for more information.

© Nursing Times

Buddhism beats depression

Should the health service sponsor Buddhist techniques to beat depression? Why not, if they work.

By Ed Halliwell

2010 could be the year that mindfulness meditation goes mainstream in the UK. It's already endorsed as a treatment for depression by the National Institute for Clinical Excellence, and today a major mental health charity is calling for meditation-based courses to be offered much more widely on the NHS.

> *Mindfulness training shows us how to notice and work with our experience rather than engaging in a futile struggle to fight or run away from it*

A report I wrote for the Mental Health Foundation highlights the impressive clinical evidence for an approach called mindfulness-based cognitive therapy (MBCT) – the eight-week courses have been shown to reduce relapse rates by half among people who have suffered several episodes of depression. The report also finds that very few patients who could benefit from mindfulness training are currently being referred for the treatment – just one in 20 GPs prescribes MBCT regularly, despite the fact that nearly three-quarters of doctors think it would be helpful for their patients with mental health problems. Changing that could make a massive difference not only to them, but to the economy – the cost of depression to the UK has been estimated at £7.5 billion every year.

Despite its convoluted name, mindfulness-based cognitive therapy is pretty straightforward – a set of classes that teach meditation practices which help people pay attention to their breathing, body sensations, thoughts and feelings in a kind, accepting, non-judgemental way. Mindfulness training shows us how to notice and work with our experience rather than engaging in a futile struggle to fight or run away from it. That may sound simple – perhaps because it is – but developing this mindful way of relating seems to alleviate some of the suffering that struggling with life's pain creates.

Mindfulness is especially relevant to depression, in which sufferers tend to get caught up with cycles of 'rumination' – when people get depressed they churn negative thoughts over and over in their minds, a pattern which actually perpetuates their low mood. Mindfulness short-circuits rumination – by learning how to pay attention to our present moment experience, rather than getting tied up in negative thinking about the past or future, we create more space in our minds from which new, more effective decision-making can emerge. It isn't a miracle cure – while simple, the techniques take time and effort to master, but mindfulness-based therapies are now supported by a substantial and rapidly-growing evidence base that suggest they can help people cope better not just with depression, but also with the stress of conditions ranging from chronic pain and anxiety to cancer and HIV.

Mindfulness-based therapies are fundamentally and unapologetically inspired by Buddhist principles and tools – the Buddha both noted that suffering (as opposed to pain) is created by struggling with experience and prescribed mindfulness meditation as a way of working with it skillfully. However, the B-word rarely, if ever, gets a mention on MBCT courses – their reputation in

So that's why he's always smiling!

THE GUARDIAN

health services has been built on scientific evidence rather than spiritual conviction. This is the only way it could be – while some of us Buddhists might argue that practising mindfulness can open up insights about the nature of mind that go way beyond what can be measured in a randomised-controlled trial, the most important thing here is that techniques which reduce suffering are presented in whatever way will make them most accessible to the largest number of people.

By secularising mindfulness training, and packaging it in a form that makes it amenable to clinical testing, an approach that might otherwise have been seen in medical circles as new-age flim-flam is being taken very seriously. So seriously that according to an ICM survey of GPs conducted for the Mental Health Foundation report, 64% of doctors would like to receive training in mindfulness themselves.

For that we can partly thank Morinaga Soko-Roshi, a zen teacher of Jon Kabat-Zinn, the doctor who first brought mindfulness training into US healthcare services in the 1970s. Kabat-Zinn knew that it would be considered unacceptably 'religious' to offer Buddhist training to his patients – however, he also had a strong hunch that the meditation techniques said to lead to insight on the Buddhist path might also help people cope with chronic illness. Unsure of what to do, he went to see

Soko-Roshi and asked his advice. 'Throw out Buddha! Throw out Zen!' came the abrupt reply.

From that, Kabat-Zinn's secular mindfulness-based stress-reduction course, a progenitor of MBCT, was born. MBSR is now taught in hundreds, perhaps thousands of institutions across the US – not just hospitals and medical settings, but schools, community centres, prisons and workplaces.

We are some way behind in the UK. Although there are now mindfulness centres at universities such as Oxford, Exeter and Bangor (the Scottish Government also deserves great credit for investing strongly in mindfulness training for health professionals), most NHS trusts lack the infrastructure and personnel to offer MBCT courses to patients who could benefit from it. Even though the scientific evidence is persuasive, and GPs are on board, there simply aren't the courses for people to access.

But with the embracing of mindfulness by a growing range of powerful institutions, whose support is based on hard-nosed evidence rather than any particular commitment to Buddhism, that may now be about to change.

5 January 2010

Antidepressants do little for mild cases

Patients with mild or moderate depression may benefit little from antidepressant medications and may be better treated with alternatives, researchers have said.

A group of researchers combined data from six studies involving 718 adult outpatients who ranged from mildly to very severely depressed according to the Hamilton Depression Rating Scale.

Their study, which sought to compare the benefits of commonly prescribed antidepressants (ADM) compared to placebos, was published in the *Journal of the American Medical Association*.

The authors, led by Jay Fournier of the University of Pennsylvania, Philadelphia, found that the effect of antidepressants varied considerably, depending on the severity of the symptoms.

'True drug effects (an advantage of ADM over placebo) were non-existent to negligible among depressed patients with mild, moderate and even severe baseline symptoms, whereas they were large for patients with very severe symptoms,' they wrote.

Most studies on antidepressants – currently the standard treatment for major depressive disorders – focus on the impact of the drugs on patients considered to be severely depressed, but there remains scant evidence on their effect for patients with less severe depression.

Advertisements for these drugs to clinicians or the general public omit this feature, the researchers noted.

The majority of patients receiving antidepressants in clinical practice have depression measures below the high level of symptom severity they found necessary for the drugs to have a meaningful impact, according to the study.

'Prescribers, policymakers and consumers may not be aware that the efficacy of medications largely has been established on the basis of studies that have included only those individuals with more severe forms of depression,' the authors wrote.

'Efforts should be made to clarify to clinicians and prospective patients that whereas antidepressant medications can have a substantial effect with more severe depressions, there is little evidence to suggest that they produce specific pharmacological benefit for the majority of patients with less severe acute depression.'

6 January 2010

THE GUARDIAN / RELAXNEWS

There's no quick fix for depression

The NHS favours pills and short-termist CBT. Life-changing therapy takes time, but could save our economy millions.

By Luiza Sauma

When it comes to depression, the British stiff upper lip is alive and well. A recent survey by the charity Turning Point reveals that three-quarters of British people experience depression at some point, making it one of the UK's most common health concerns. Despite its prevalence, a third of sufferers do not seek help due to embarrassment, worries about confidentiality and a feeling that they could cope by themselves.

Turning Point's findings are depressingly familiar to me. As well as being a journalist, I work part-time as a parents' helpline adviser at the mental health charity YoungMinds, where depression is the most common theme of the calls – even if the 'D' word is never mentioned. Some of these calls are carbon copies of each other – the names, locations and social classes change, but the story remains the same: a young person has dropped out of education or employment, they've stopped seeing their friends; they can't even get out of bed or hold down an undemanding part-time job. Why, ask many parents, won't they just pull themselves together?

I'm originally from Brazil, where chatting openly about your emotions, problems and, indeed, your psychotherapist (among the middle classes, at least) is *de rigueur*. But I was brought up in Britain, where depression is rarely out of the news, yet is often treated with a mixture of suspicion, contempt and shame. It's not just young Neets (not in employment, education or training) who are falling prey to it – although one could be rather superficial and say that, what with today's job market, they have the most to be miserable about.

Depression is, of course, much more than just status anxiety. From Alexander McQueen's death to Dolly Parton's recent revelation that she had been suicidal in the 1980s, every week another gifted and admired public figure is revealed to have suffered from crippling misery. Artists, writers and performers, however, have a get-out clause: they are allowed to express their dark sides, so we don't have to.

Around 31 million prescriptions for antidepressants are doled out every year to the British public. After all, pills – like cognitive behavioural therapy – are cheap, and fit neatly into the idea that a depression is a 'chemical imbalance' that can be easily cured. The psychiatrist and psychoanalyst Dr John Steiner tells me that the chemical imbalance idea can be 'damaging, but it's partly true. Some people are just more prone to depression than others. But then there's also an interaction of that person's genetic make-up with their relationships.' According to Steiner, CBT 'can often work in the short term, but it doesn't affect the underlying problem. It's a symptom-treatment, like antidepressants.'

Longer-term psychotherapy aims to uncover those underlying problems. But as anyone with depression will know, getting referred on the NHS to anything other than CBT is almost impossible. On the YoungMinds helpline, I've even heard of young people being offered electroconvulsive therapy before talking therapy – one would think that it would be the last, not the first or second, resort.

Imagine if you had cancer and you couldn't get referred to a life-saving treatment. Like cancer, depression kills people and destroys lives – not just of sufferers, but of their families too. Just as there are different types of cancer, there are different types of depression. I suffered a relatively mild version a couple of years ago and I was at pains to disguise it: after all, I had a fantastic job at a newspaper, a wonderful boyfriend and loving, supportive family and friends – what did I have to be miserable about?

A friend of mine has suffered from a more aggressive form of the illness. 'It feels like walking through treacle,' she said. 'Everyday tasks seem exhausting and impossible, people terrifying and hostile, and life an endless desert of weariness and despair.' Unlike me, she's been through the mill of NHS mental health services, has gulped down the antidepressants and tried CBT, to little or no avail.

'It too often seems like an admittance of weakness, in a way that having a broken arm or gastric flu just doesn't,' she admits. 'I've felt very, very patronised by GPs. Being asked questions like, "Do you feel worthless?" or "Do you feel suicidal?" in a form-filling monotone is somewhat dispiriting. It's hard to be strong and assertive when you're suffering. And often that's what you need, when services are very hard to access.'

In short, people who cannot afford private treatment are being locked out by a system that favours cheap, temporary fixes over long-term results. Yes, access to proper treatment for depression – the kind that can actually change one's life – would be a drain to the economy, but so are all the depressed, under-supported people who make up the majority of incapacity benefit claimants.

Economically, it could make perfect sense, if a more productive, happier Britain was within our grasp.

17 February 2010

THE GUARDIAN

What can I do to help myself?

Helping yourself, or self-help, is a great place to start. It involves figuring out what changes you can make in your own life to help improve your mood. It's all about what YOU can do for YOU.

'To me self-help is about being proactive and finding out what there is available to help me. I see a psychologist and take antidepressants but for me this is not enough – I need more if I am to get in control of my depression.'
Alasdair

It's a bit like what Alasdair says in his quote, the value of self-help is that you don't need to rely on other people. You get to take control of your situation and take charge of what you do: learn a new skill; have some fun; do stuff that's good for you. Your choice.

You could try the following tips:

Talk to someone you trust

You really are not alone. Talking about how you feel is one of the best things you can do if you are concerned about your low mood or anxiety. A problem shared is a problem eased and all that – but talking really can help you feel less alone with your problems. Not that it is always easy. A lot of people will find it hard, and the first time you tell someone about how you are feeling might be really difficult. If you feel you can't talk to friends or family, then talk to your GP or contact a helpline. There are people who are ready to listen or just be on the other end of the phone when you need them.

While everyone's experience of low mood, depression and anxiety will be different, talking to other people is a really useful way of getting support. It can be a relief to find out that other people have similar worries and concerns and you aren't the only one to feel this way. You might know someone else who suffers from low mood, depression or anxiety – by sharing stories of your experience you can learn what strategies worked for them. Even just the process of writing down your experiences can make you feel better. Check out the stories on www.lookokfeelcrap.org in 'Is it just me?', and there are heaps of quotes dotted on the site that have come from people who have depression and have contacted us for help. Send us an email to ask@lookokfeelcrap.org

Exercise

People who exercise tend to feel happier and more satisfied with their lives than those who are inactive. It's a fact! A large general public survey done in the UK found that physical exercise was rated as the most effective way of improving low mood. And there is evidence now to back this up. Studies have shown that exercise can prevent depression from occurring and stop it from coming back.

But all things in moderation! If you haven't done any exercise for a while don't go crazy with it and start training every day. Or if you have any other health concerns that make it more difficult to exercise, like ME, then it's best to talk to your GP or a trainer about what would be best. It's important that you build your fitness up slowly so that you don't get too tired and give up, or cause yourself any injuries. Start off by doing something gentle, like walking or swimming. Over time you can get into running, team sports, adventure sports or whatever it is you most enjoy.

> **Talking about how you feel is one of the best things you can do if you are concerned about your low mood**

The Depression Alliance Scotland website has a page on how exercise can improve your mood, including links to useful resources and information that might get you going. Visit: www.dascot.org/exercise.html

Inspirational and self-help books

You might find reading self-help or inspirational books a helpful way of finding out more information about mood and anxiety and how to overcome emotional problems. Self-help books range from personal accounts of living with mental health problems to more structured course workbooks where you learn techniques and fill in set tasks.

It is becoming more common for doctors and health clinics to suggest books to people experiencing low mood. This is called bibliotherapy. Ask at your local health centre if this service is available to you.

Depression Alliance Scotland has a books page on their website with a list of books that people have found helpful: www.dascot.org/books.htm. If you've read a self-help book that you found helpful and want to write a review, then send it in to us and we can post it on our website. Email us at: ask@lookokfeelcrap.org

LOOK OK... FEEL CRAP?

Doing something you enjoy and REWARD yourself

This might sound obvious, but it is quite common for people with depression to stop doing the things that they most enjoy doing. Tiredness, feelings of not being bothered and wanting to hide away often all conspire and you end up doing less and less and seeing fewer and fewer people. It can be tough to convince yourself to get out of the house and do it, but planning activities that you used to enjoy will help you keep up a regular routine and in contact with other people. Invite your friends to join you if you need some added motivation. As with exercise, don't be too adventurous – plan things that are manageable for you and increase them slowly over time. Things you could try:

⇨ Meeting a friend for a drink.

⇨ Going to the movies.

⇨ Getting creative – writing, sewing, painting, photography.

⇨ Joining a book group or a similar interest group.

⇨ Taking music classes.

⇨ Enjoying a bath.

⇨ Learning to relax by having a massage, facial, doing yoga or meditation.

⇨ Listening to music. Playing an instrument!

⇨ … Whatever it is that you will ENJOY.

Learn to recognise your own successes. It can be easy to compare yourself with your friends and feel that what you are doing is not worth anything, but if you are coping with depression, everything is much harder and any achievement, no matter how big or small, is worth noting.

Improving sleep

It is common to have sleeping difficulties and it can be tempting to turn night into day. This can make things worse, so try to have regular sleeping and eating times, even if it is hard to get to sleep. Here are some tips:

⇨ Don't worry about it. As hard as it seems, worrying about not sleeping just makes it even harder to get to sleep. If you've got a lot on your mind and a busy day/week ahead try writing a 'to do' list before you go to bed. Also, write down the next step you need to take to progress them. That will hopefully put them out of your mind for the night.

⇨ If you find yourself thinking over things while in bed, tell yourself that you've got it under control and will deal with it in the morning. If your worries are really persistent, write them down. Keep a notepad beside your bed so that it's handy.

⇨ Don't lie in bed for more than 30 minutes when you can't sleep. Get up. Walk around your room. Make yourself a camomile tea or milky drink. Do something calm and relaxing. Head back to bed and see if that helps.

⇨ Turn your mobile off. Being woken up by a text in the wee early hours ain't going to help!

⇨ Don't stay up late on the computer. In fact, don't do anything that is going to stimulate your brain immediately before going to bed. Computers and TV are not a good idea, as the flashing pictures and colours just keep your brain alert.

⇨ Limit naps during the day. Every hour you sleep during the day will mean more time you are awake at night, so unless you have another health condition which means you need more sleep than on average, resist the temptation.

⇨ Establish regular times for going to bed and getting up, so that your body and brain recognise when it is time for sleep.

⇨ Doing physical exercise during the day can help you get a good night's sleep, but try not to exercise within two hours of going to bed. Exercise sends endorphins around your body which act as a stimulant.

⇨ Avoid eating heavy meals just before going to bed as well. Your digestive system will need to work hard to digest the food, and to do this it needs to keep your body alert. A warm milky drink or herbal tea such as camomile, which is supposed to induce sleep, can be helpful though. Our brain often mistakes thirst for hunger, and we end up snacking when our body just needs some water – so try a drink before food.

⇨ It can be hard to resist drinking coffee, coke and energy drinks during the day if you're already tired but this can make your sleep problem worse. All of these drinks have high levels of caffeine in them, which will keep you awake. Watch what you snack on as well – chocolate has caffeine in it, especially the dark stuff! Maybe set a cut-off time during the afternoon when you won't have any more and try and stick to it.

⇨ Same goes with alcohol and cigarettes. While you might think that they help calm you, they can make sleep problems worse. Nicotine is a stimulant, and alcohol disrupts sleep, causing you to wake more easily. Not least of all because you need to pee more.

⇨ The above information is reprinted with kind permission from Look OK... Feel Crap? Visit www.lookokfeelcrap.org for more information.

© Depression Alliance Scotland

LOOK OK... FEEL CRAP?

KEY FACTS

⇨ Depression affects a person's physical state, mood and thought processes. People with depression cannot merely 'pull themselves together' and get better. It is not a sign of personal weakness or a condition that can be willed away but an illness that needs treatment to reduce symptoms. (page 1)

⇨ Mood change and depression are more common in people suffering from physical illnesses than in people who are well. (page 3)

⇨ You're three times more likely to develop depression if your parents suffered depression, but it's not inevitable. Scientists believe the risk of developing depression results from a combination of genetic, biochemical, psychological and environmental factors. (page 4)

⇨ 75% of people in the UK suffer from depression at some time in their lives, but only a third seek help, research has found. (page 5)

⇨ Depression affects one in five older people living in the community and two in five living in care homes. (page 7)

⇨ Depression is far more than the feeling of being fed up and miserable that everyone experiences. You feel useless, desperate, guilty, hopeless and unable to think properly. You may find it difficult, if not impossible, to do the ordinary things of everyday life. (page 8)

⇨ Major mood disorders affect 20 per cent of the population and are among the leading causes of disability worldwide. (page 12)

⇨ People who suffer from depression and mania are more likely to focus on success, money and fame than others, research has found. (page 13)

⇨ 25% of people aged over 55 surveyed believed that it downgraded neighbourhoods when someone with a mental illness began living there. (page 16)

⇨ Just 14% of men (35–44 years old) would see a GP if they felt low compared to 37% of women. (page 18)

⇨ A study by researchers at the University of Bergen, Norway, and the Institute of Psychiatry (IoP) at King's College London has found that depression is as much of a risk factor for mortality as smoking. (page 20)

⇨ For people with severe depression, the lifetime risk of suicide may be as high as 6%. This compares with a risk of 1.3% in the general population. (page 21)

⇨ In total, about one in six adults are known to have a neurotic mental health disorder in any given week. The most common disorder is mixed anxiety and depression (8.8%). (page 22)

⇨ In western Europe the prevalence for post-natal depression is 13%. (page 23)

⇨ Depression usually starts between the ages of 15 and 30. (page 25)

⇨ Incidence of attempted suicide and self-mutilation is higher in females than males while completed suicide is higher in males. One of the most vulnerable groups for completed suicide is the 18–24 age group. (page 26)

⇨ 1.7% of 16- to 19-year-olds and 2.2% of 20- to 24-year-olds, or about 127,000, have suffered from a depressive episode. (page 27)

⇨ There was no rise in the level of emotional problems such as anxiety and depression amongst 11- to 15-year-olds between 1999 and 2004. In the same period there was a slight decrease in the level of conduct problems such as lying and disobedience. This follows a 25-year period in which the rate of all these problems had risen dramatically (from 1974 to 1999). (page 30)

⇨ GPs have difficulty recognising depression in their patients, according to an overview of more than 40 studies conducted by the University of Leicester. The research, involving more than 50,000 patients, found that GPs correctly picked up on depression in only 50% of cases. They were actually more likely to misdiagnose a patient as depressed than they were to spot a case of genuine depression. (page 31)

⇨ Nearly three-quarters of people in the UK experience depression occasionally, according to a recent survey from Turning Point. The mental health charity found that of these, only a third will actually seek help. (page 33)

⇨ Patients with mild or moderate depression may benefit little from antidepressant medications and may be better treated with alternatives, researchers have said. (page 36)

Antidepressants

These include tricyclic antidepressants (TCAs), selective serotonin re-uptake inhibitors (SSRIs) and monoamine oxidase inhibitors (MAOIs). Antidepressants work by boosting one or more chemicals (neurotransmitters) in the nervous system, which may be present in insufficient amounts during a depressive illness.

Antipsychotic drugs

These are sometimes used to treat bipolar disorder sufferers during periods of mania. They have a sedative effect and aim to relieve the distressing symptoms associated with manic states.

Bipolar disorder

Previously called manic depression, this illness is characterised by mood swings where periods of severe depression are balanced by periods of elation and overactivity (mania).

Cognitive behavioural therapy (CBT)

A psychological treatment that assumes that behavioural and emotional reactions are learned over a long period. A cognitive therapist will seek to identify the source of emotional problems and develop techniques to overcome them.

Depression

Someone is said to be significantly depressed, or suffering from depression, when feelings of sadness or misery don't go away quickly and are so bad that they interfere with everyday life. Symptoms can also include low self-esteem and a lack of motivation.

Electroconvulsive therapy (ECT)

A treatment for depression which involves a brief electrical stimulus given to the brain via electrodes placed on the temples.

Endogenous depression

Not always triggered by an upsetting or stressful event. Sufferers may experience weight change, tiredness, sleeping problems, low mood, poor concentration and low self-esteem.

Light therapy

A treatment for seasonal affective disorder (SAD) which involves sitting near a light box for up to an hour a day.

Post-natal depression

Depression experienced by new mothers. It is not known for certain what causes it, but some experts believe the sudden change in hormones after a baby's birth may be the trigger. Symptoms may include panic attacks, sleeping difficulties, overwhelming fear of death and feelings of inadequacy/being unable to cope.

Puerperal psychosis

This is the most extreme form of mental illness new mums can suffer from after the birth of a baby. It's very rare, affecting just one in 500 new mums. Symptoms experienced can include hallucinations, agitation, confusion and even urges to harm oneself or the baby.

Reactive depression

Depression triggered by a traumatic, difficult or stressful event, or following a prolonged period of stress. Sufferers may feel low, anxious, irritable or angry.

Seasonal affective disorder (SAD)

A type of depression which generally coincides with the approach of winter and is linked to shortening of daylight hours and lack of sunlight.

St John's Wort (Hypericum)

A yellow-flowered plant that has been used for centuries as a mild antidepressant.

Talking therapies

These involve talking and listening. Some therapists will aim to find the root cause of a sufferer's problem and help them deal with it, some will help to change behaviour and negative thoughts, while others simply offer support.

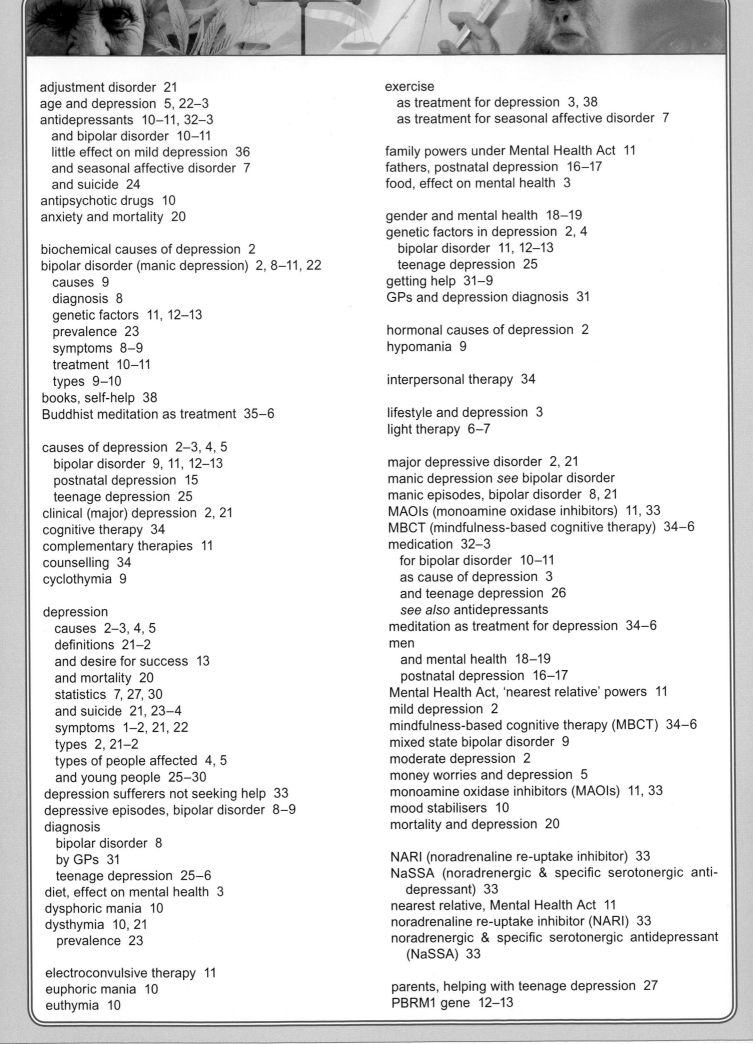

adjustment disorder 21
age and depression 5, 22–3
antidepressants 10–11, 32–3
   and bipolar disorder 10–11
   little effect on mild depression 36
   and seasonal affective disorder 7
   and suicide 24
antipsychotic drugs 10
anxiety and mortality 20

biochemical causes of depression 2
bipolar disorder (manic depression) 2, 8–11, 22
   causes 9
   diagnosis 8
   genetic factors 11, 12–13
   prevalence 23
   symptoms 8–9
   treatment 10–11
   types 9–10
books, self-help 38
Buddhist meditation as treatment 35–6

causes of depression 2–3, 4, 5
   bipolar disorder 9, 11, 12–13
   postnatal depression 15
   teenage depression 25
clinical (major) depression 2, 21
cognitive therapy 34
complementary therapies 11
counselling 34
cyclothymia 9

depression
   causes 2–3, 4, 5
   definitions 21–2
   and desire for success 13
   and mortality 20
   statistics 7, 27, 30
   and suicide 21, 23–4
   symptoms 1–2, 21, 22
   types 2, 21–2
   types of people affected 4, 5
   and young people 25–30
depression sufferers not seeking help 33
depressive episodes, bipolar disorder 8–9
diagnosis
   bipolar disorder 8
   by GPs 31
   teenage depression 25–6
diet, effect on mental health 3
dysphoric mania 10
dysthymia 10, 21
   prevalence 23

electroconvulsive therapy 11
euphoric mania 10
euthymia 10

exercise
   as treatment for depression 3, 38
   as treatment for seasonal affective disorder 7

family powers under Mental Health Act 11
fathers, postnatal depression 16–17
food, effect on mental health 3

gender and mental health 18–19
genetic factors in depression 2, 4
   bipolar disorder 11, 12–13
   teenage depression 25
getting help 31–9
GPs and depression diagnosis 31

hormonal causes of depression 2
hypomania 9

interpersonal therapy 34

lifestyle and depression 3
light therapy 6–7

major depressive disorder 2, 21
manic depression see bipolar disorder
manic episodes, bipolar disorder 8, 21
MAOIs (monoamine oxidase inhibitors) 11, 33
MBCT (mindfulness-based cognitive therapy) 34–6
medication 32–3
   for bipolar disorder 10–11
   as cause of depression 3
   and teenage depression 26
   see also antidepressants
meditation as treatment for depression 34–6
men
   and mental health 18–19
   postnatal depression 16–17
Mental Health Act, 'nearest relative' powers 11
mild depression 2
mindfulness-based cognitive therapy (MBCT) 34–6
mixed state bipolar disorder 9
moderate depression 2
money worries and depression 5
monoamine oxidase inhibitors (MAOIs) 11, 33
mood stabilisers 10
mortality and depression 20

NARI (noradrenaline re-uptake inhibitor) 33
NaSSA (noradrenergic & specific serotonergic antidepressant) 33
nearest relative, Mental Health Act 11
noradrenaline re-uptake inhibitor (NARI) 33
noradrenergic & specific serotonergic antidepressant
   (NaSSA) 33

parents, helping with teenage depression 27
PBRM1 gene 12–13

Additional Resources

Other Issues titles

If you are interested in researching further some of the issues raised in *Coping with Depression,* you may like to read the following titles in the **Issues** series:

⇨ Vol. 192 *Bereavement and Grief* (ISBN 978 1 86168 543 8)

⇨ Vol. 186 *Cannabis Use* (ISBN 978 1 86168 527 8)

⇨ Vol. 165 *Bullying Issues* (ISBN 978 1 86168 469 1)

⇨ Vol. 141 *Mental Health* (ISBN 978 1 86168 407 3)

⇨ Vol. 136 *Self-Harm* (ISBN 978 1 86168 388 5)

⇨ Vol. 100 *Stress and Anxiety* (ISBN 978 1 86168 314 4)

For a complete list of available **Issues** titles, please visit our website: www.independence.co.uk/shop

Useful organisations

You may find the websites of the following organisations useful for further research:

⇨ **Depression Alliance Scotland:** www.dascot.org

⇨ **Look OK... Feel Crap?:** www.lookokfeelcrap.org

⇨ **MDF:** www.mdf.org.uk

⇨ **Mental Health Foundation:** www.mentalhealth.org.uk

⇨ **Mind:** www.mind.org.uk

⇨ **Nuffield Foundation:** www.nuffieldfoundation.org

⇨ **Rethink:** www.rethink.org

⇨ **Samaritans:** www.samaritans.org

⇨ **Turning Point:** www.turning-point.co.uk

⇨ **YoungMinds:** www.youngminds.org.uk

ACKNOWLEDGEMENTS

The publisher is grateful for permission to reproduce the following material.

While every care has been taken to trace and acknowledge copyright, the publisher tenders its apology for any accidental infringement or where copyright has proved untraceable. The publisher would be pleased to come to a suitable arrangement in any such case with the rightful owner.

Chapter One: About Depression

Depression, © Rethink, *Myths about depression quiz,* © 2009 WebMD, LLC. All rights reserved, *Depression affects three out of four in UK,* © Nursing Times, *Seasonal Affective Disorder (SAD) or winter depression,* © Depression Alliance Scotland, *Statistics on mental health,* © Mental Health Foundation, *Bipolar as a condition,* © MDF, *Same genes suspected in both depression and bipolar illness,* © NIMH, *Depression linked to desire for fame, say scientists,* © Telegraph Media Group Limited 2010, *Post-natal depression,* © Bounty, *Likelihood of going to GP for help about a mental health problem [graph],* © Crown copyright is reproduced with the permission of Her Majesty's Stationery Office, *How comfortable would you feel talking to a friend or family member about your mental health? [graph],* © Crown copyright is reproduced with the permission of Her Majesty's Stationery Office, *News dads get depressed too,* © Nick Duerden, *Fear and exclusion of people with mental illness, by age [graph],* © Crown copyright is reproduced with the permission of Her Majesty's Stationery Office, *Men and mental health: get it off your chest,* © Mind, *Suicide rates by gender: 1998, 2007-08, United Kingdom [graph],* © Crown copyright is reproduced with the permission of Her Majesty's Stationery Office, *Depression as deadly as smoking but anxiety may be good for you,* © Institute of Psychiatry, King's College London, *Depression and suicide,* © Samaritans, *Suicide rates in the UK 1991-2008 [graph],* © Crown copyright is reproduced with the permission of Her Majesty's Stationery Office.

Chapter Two: Depression and Young People

Teenage depression, © 2009 WebMD, LLC. All rights reserved, *Statistics about young adults with mental health problems,* © YoungMinds, *Living with depression,* © youthhealthtalk.org, *Teenage depression no longer on the increase,* © Nuffield Foundation.

Chapter Three: Diagnosis and Treatment

When a seven-minute diagnosis is not enough, © Guardian News and Media Limited 2009, *Antidepressants,* © TheSite, *Depression sufferers 'not seeking help',* © Turning Point, *Talking treatment,* © Depression Alliance Scotland, *NHS should use meditation to treat depression, says report,* © Nursing Times, *Buddhism beats depression,* © Guardian News and Media Limited 2010, *Antidepressants do little for mild cases,* © relaxnews: www.relaxnews.com, *There's no quick fix for depression,* © Guardian News and Media Limited 2010, *What can I do to help myself?,* © Depression Alliance Scotland.

Illustrations

Pages 1, 12, 20, 30: Simon Kneebone; pages 3, 15, 23, 35: Angelo Madrid; pages 6, 17a, 17b, 26: Don Hatcher; pages 10, 18: Bev Aisbett.

Cover photography

Left: © Marc Garrido i Puig. Centre: © Sanja Gjenero. Right: © Kriss Szkurlatowski.

Additional acknowledgements

Research by Sabrine Paupiah.

Additional research by Hart McLeod Limited, Cambridge.

With thanks to the Independence team: Mary Chapman, Sandra Dennis and Jan Sunderland.

Lisa Firth
Cambridge
May, 2010